estrogenius 2012
a celebration of female voices

Plays

Cover Design: Melissa Riker ♦ Editor: Anne Carlino

Published by PlaySource
A division of manhattantheatresource

Table of Contents

Plays

GROUP **A**

GROUP **B**

GROUP **C**

Introduction

We did it! 2012 was a watershed year for the festival. Our 13th year and the 1st one produced outside of our former Greenwich Village space. Held at TBG Theatre on W. 36th St., the festival included all the components our audiences have come to know and love: short plays, solo shows, music, visual art, dance, teen performances, and stand-up comedy.

Theatre is, by its nature, collaborative, and EstroGenius is a showcase of collaboration at its very best. We start with a team of committed producers, and we add great scripts, inspired directors, talented actors, magical designers, supercompetent stage managers, and a flock of other volunteer support. The result is a festival that is absolutely first-rate and gets better every year.

The scripts alone — great as they are — can never fully encapsulate all that the festival is, but it can certainly give you a sense of the solid foundation we build upon. Enjoy!

And, if you like what you read, please consider a donation (tax-deductible of course.)

See you at the next one!

Jen Thatcher, Executive Producer, EstroGenius

Executive Director, Manhattan Theatre Source

ManhattanTheatreSource ("the Source") is a not-for-profit arts producing organization with a groundbreaking purpose: To link the disparate communities within New York's vital off-off-Broadway movement, and to provide resources for independent theatre artists and audiences.

For 12 years, the Source operated a multi-use performance space in the heart of Greenwich Village. Beginning in 2000, the Source proudly honored Off-Off Broadway's Greenwich Village roots by creating a home for artists of all disciplines and offering a playground for passion and mistakes, hard work and cooperation, big ideas and small budgets. At the end of 2011, we made the difficult decision to close our doors and become one of the thousands of passionate arts production companies that operate without owning a performance space. As hard as that decision was, it has freed us to focus on the creation of art and artistic opportunities, which has always been at the heart of what we do.

Nurturing artists of all levels, the Source has been and continues to be a launching pad for dozens of successful artists, companies and projects, which have gone on to the Fringe, Off-Broadway runs and even the Great White Way — the 2006 Obie Award-winning musical [title of show] had its first ever production in our space, and went on to its Broadway debut in July 2008 at the Lyceum.

And, with or without a performance space, we always operate by the principles of our four House Rules:
- Practice generosity of spirit
- Share your information
- Principles before personalities
- Clean up after yourself

If what you've just read sounds intriguing, come join us. There's always more room in our sandbox for those interested in creating art...but keeping the drama onstage.

Festival Staff

FOUNDING PRODUCER: Fiona Jones

EXECUTIVE PRODUCER: Jen Thatcher

ASSISTANT EXECUTIVE PRODUCER: Anne Carlino

SHORT PLAY PRODUCERS: Jen Thatcher, Catie Choate, and Andi Cohen

SHORT PLAY ASSISTANT PRODUCERS: Anne Carlino, Earline Stephen, Margaret Stockton

WOMEN IN MOTION PRODUCERS: Melissa Riker, Amber Sloan, Esther Palmer, Anne Zuerner

GIRL BE HEARD: Producer: Jessica Greer Morris, Artist-in Residence: Winter Miller, Directed by Ashley Marinaccio

SOLA VOCE PRODUCER: Cheryl King

VISUAL ARTS CURATOR: Heidi Russell

LIGHTING DIRECTOR: Kia Rogers

REHEARSAL SPACE COORDINATOR: Anne Carlino

MARKETING DIRECTOR: Malini Singh-McDonald

SUBMISSIONS COORDINATOR: Michael Bordwell

STAND-UP for ESTRO! PRODUCER: Maribeth Mooney

MASTER ELECTRICIAN: Sam Gordon

TECHNICAL DIRECTOR: Liz Torres

SET DESIGNER: Sandy Yaklin

MUSIC COORDINATOR: Christa Victoria

Submission Reviewers: Francesca Aquino, Lauren Arneson, Donna Barkman, Dev Bondarin, Jennifer Bronstein, Anne Carlino, Sarah Chichester, Angela Theresa Collins, Sonia da Silva, Alejandra Diaz, Sarah Doudna, C. J. Erlich, Charlie Fersko, Helene Galek, Hannah Gold, Alaina Hammond, Sheila Joon, Christine Kestner, Bill Kozy, Annalisa Loeffler, Jessica McVea, Barbara Mundy, Mary Murphy, Vivian Neuwirth, Kathleen O'Neill, Jenny Paul, Ellie Pyle, Emily Rupp, Jessica Sharples, & Margaret Stockton

Acknowledgments

Super-Huge Thanks to our Donors —
You made the 2012 Festival possible!

Leigh Angel, David Asbury & Kara Dansky, John Bodamer, Daryl Boling, Anthony Call, Laura Camien, Anne Carlino, Nat Cassidy, Wendy Caster, Clare Cooper, Carissa Cordes, Sonia da Silva, Alexandra de Suze, Amy Dickenson, Lisa Dillman, Sarah Doudna, Susie & Dave Ecklunk, C. J. Ehrlich, Ato Essandoh, Littith Fallon, Jessica Fleitman, Andrew Frank, Jen Friedlander, Homer Frizzell, FUNNY...SHEESH PRODUCTIONS, Gabriel Furman, Helene Galek, Hope Garlkand, Martha Garvey, Kathryn Gerhardt, Anita Gonzalez, John R. Harvey, Sheila Head, Debra Henri, Jason Howard, Mavis L. Johnson, Paige Jonston, Nataniel Kassel & Zahara Wignot, Paula J. Kelly, Christine Kestner, Krista Knight, Jessica Knutson, William Kozy, Doug Krehbel,Nancy Lapid, Jennifer Lindsay, Annalisa Lieffler, Deborah Long, Susan Lyles/And ToTo Too Theatre Co., Edmond Malin, Vincent Marano, Malini McDonald, John McLaughlin, Jessica McVea, Michelle Miller, Maribeth Mooney, Jessica Morris, Walter Nacnodovitz, Edward Neuwirth, Vivian Neuwirth, Ridley Parson, Jennifer Paul, Christie Perfetti, Julie Perkins, Laurie Petersen, Laura Pruden, Matthew Quint & Tegan Culler, Catie Riggs, Melissa Riker, Johnny Rodriguez, David Rogers, Kia Rogers, Lisa Roth, Lisa Rothe, Heidi Russell, Melanie Ryan, John Schoneboom, Llaurie Schoreder, Teddy Sears, Doug Silver, Franny Silverman, Barbara Slavin & Art Bushkin, Rob Staeger, Margaret Stockton, Dorian Stone, Ann Strohm, Michael Swalina, Carla Tassara, Adina Taubman, Jen & Jesse Thatcher, Jesse & Donna Thatcher,Jennifer Gordon Thomas, Shannon Ward, Jamilia Wignot, Shaun Wilson, Saundra Yaklin, Shey Lyn Zanotti &
Anonymous

§

Special Thanks
To our participating artists, technical, production, and administrative staff, and especially:

Michael Roderick, Small Pond Enterprises
Zach Wobensmith
Shetler Studios
The Producers' Club
&
Stage Left Productions

Copyrights and Permissions

A Recipe to Remember

by Celeste Koehler

Produced by manhattan**theatre**source *in Group A of EstroGenius 2012 with the following cast and crew:*

Director: Estefania Fadul

Monica: Marianne Ferrari*

Deirdre: Mary Matoula Webb

Mother: Donna Barkman*

Sound Designer: Amber Gallery

Lighting Designer: Kayla Goble

Stage Manager: Katt Masterson

Costume Designer: Julija Frodina

*Member of Actors' Equity Association

CONTACT
celestekoehler54@gmail.com

CHARACTERS

MONICA – female, early to mid forties.

DEIRDRE – female, late thirties to mid forties, younger sister to MONICA

MOTHER – female, Mother of MONICA and DEIRDRE. Sixty or more. Suffers with Alzheimer's disease.

Setting: DEIRDRE'S kitchen

Time: morning

At Rise: Upstage is a coatrack, with a coat hanging on it. There is a table and three chairs at Center stage. An elderly woman sits at the table in the center. She is dressed strangely as though dressed by a child. She wears two sweaters over her dress, the outer one mis-buttoned. She wears two pairs of panty hose but only one leg in each pair with the other leg dangling down her legs. She has on one shoe and a house slipper. On the table are various paper napkins and tissues that the woman occupies herself with folding and unfolding and refolding throughout the play. At times throughout the play she can be heard softly humming. Also on the table are a covered bowl of applesauce and several spoons, a pot of coffee and two cups.

(Enter MONICA, *removes coat, hangs it on coat rack.)*

MONICA: Deirdre! Deirdre, where are you?
(Walks over to MOTHER *and kisses her)*
   How are you today, Mom?
(Looks over her clothes, picks up one of the dangling hose)
   Dressed yourself, I see.

(Enter DEIRDRE*)*

DEIRDRE: She was up at the crack of dawn. No, I take that back. She was up all night. We were all up all night.

MONICA: You sounded hysterical on the phone, what's going on?
(She pours herself a cup of coffee)

DEIRDRE: *(Approaches* MOTHER, *unbuttons sweater and buttons   correctly)*
   Dan just left for work and I wouldn't be surprised if he never came home again.

MONICA : *(Sitting)* Business that good?

DEIRDRE: No, life at home that bad.
(Picks up dangling hose and shakes her head in resignation, then drops it)
   Monica, you know why I called, I just can't take any more.

MONICA: Okay, okay tell me what happened.

DEIRDRE: This morning she got into her closet, she took out everything, it looked like the room had been ransacked. Then she put on half the clothes she owns. She must have at least four undershirts on under those sweaters. She just keeps piling clothes on, one on top of the other.

MONICA: Maybe she's cold. How'd she get out of bed anyway? I thought the side-rails were supposed to keep her in bed.

DEIRDRE: She's figured out how to climb over them. Don't ask me how. When she sets her mind on something, there's no stopping her. Monica, I've had it, I can't take anymore.

MONICA: Well, buck up, girl. You've got three more weeks to go. I'm not taking her one day early. You just have to stick it out until then and then you have three months of normal life again. Steve is already getting grumpy in anticipation of her arrival.

DEIRDRE: *(Desperate)*
Monica, you're not listening. I'm losing my mind, I'm losing my marriage, I'm serious here.

MONICA: *(Stands, approaches DEIRDRE)* Why? Deirdre, what is it?

DEIRDRE: I'm... I'm not sure I can even tell you.

MONICA: Don't be ridiculous! I'm your sister. You can tell me anything.

DEIRDRE: It's so embarrassing.

MONICA: Nothing is so embarrassing you can't talk about it to your sister.
(Beat)
Unless it's about sex.

DEIRDRE: Well...

MONICA: Oh, I see. Nothing like having the mother-in-law in the next room to put a damper on a man's ardor. I get ya. But I'm not going to help you. Even your dismal sex life won't guilt me into taking her early. My sex life is great, by the way. Steve's trying to get it all in before she arrives. I just hope I have the energy to take her when the time comes.

DEIRDRE: Monica! I don't give a flying fuck about your sex life! I'm worried about my marriage for god's sake!

MONICA: De!? Watch your language! You want her coming out with that the next time you're at the grocery store? What's got you so upset? Just tell me.

DEIRDRE: *(Facing* MOTHER*)* Sorry, Mom.
(Sighs, addressing MONICA*)*
Dan was away, you know, on a business trip.

MONICA: Yeah...

DEIRDRE: So, you know how it is. We were looking forward to being alone together. I got Mom in bed, got the kids settled early. We were looking forward to a romantic night.

MONICA: Yeah...

DEIRDRE: So, there we were, alone, in bed, making love.

MOTHER: Yeah...

(They turn and look at MOTHER *momentarily, move a few steps out of earshot)*

MONICA: And?

DEIRDRE: And the bed's bouncing up and down in ecstasy...and all of a sudden we realize we're not alone.

MONICA: What?

DEIRDRE: She was there, Monica. Dan flicked on the light and there she was, sitting on the end of our bed bouncing away.

MONICA: O...My....God!

DEIRDRE: Dan jumps up, naked, out of the bed, trips over the dog. Mom, of course, was terrified, she starts wailing, the dog's barking, Dan's screaming, the kids wake up and come running into our room. It was an absolute freaking nightmare!

MONICA: *(Laughing)* O My God, Deirdre! That's too much! The girls at Mah Jong will never believe this!

DEIRDRE: Monica! It's not funny.

MONICA: *(Still laughing)* Yes, it is. I'd have given anything to see your face. I have this mental picture that will never go away. Oh, poor Dan.

DEIRDRE: Last night was the worst night of my life. How can you laugh about it, Monica? You always think the stuff she does is funny. You're so insensitive. Our mother has lost her mind and you're laughing about it.

MONICA: What else do you want me to do, Deirdre? I don't see a lot of options here. I laugh because I have to, it's the only thing that keeps the pain away. You might try it, by the way, maybe you'll cope a little better.

(MONICA moves to table and sits beside MOTHER)

DEIRDRE: My face? *(Starts laughing)* You should have seen Dan's! O God,
(Moves to table sits at the end of it)
This stupid, horrible disease, how are we ever going to survive this?

MONICA: We're not, De. Not the way we're going about it. We can't keep doing this to ourselves and our families. We have to place her, we can't avoid it anymore.

DEIRDRE: No, Monica! We agreed! She took care of us our whole lives. This is the least we can do for her.

MONICA: Deirdre, it's time.

DEIRDRE: *(Jumps up)* I can't do it. I can't put her into a home. We can't just hand her over to be cared for by a bunch of strangers.

MONICA: *(Standing)* Strangers? For God's sake, Deirdre, what does it matter? She doesn't know who we are. We're all strangers to her. When's the last time she called you by name? When was it?

DEIRDRE: I don't know.

MONICA: Six months, a year?

DEIRDRE: *(Sitting)* I don't know.

MONICA: *(Sighs deeply, returns to her seat)*
Last time she was with us, I asked Jill to take her into the bathroom and help her brush her teeth. At first I heard Jill laugh, but when I went in to check on them, there was Jill, holding mother's slimy teeth in her hand, while mother was busy with the toothbrush trying to scrub a mole off her leg. And my daughter just stood there with tears streaming down her face, watching this stranger who used to be her grandmother... You want to know why I laugh? It's so I don't have to think about moments like that.

DEIRDRE: You never told me about that. Poor Jill.

MONICA: And then she wanted to know, 'Are you going to get it too, Mom? Is this going to happen to you?'

DEIRDRE: Oh, Monica, what did you say to her?

MONICA: What could I say? I told her, 'of course not. It skips a generation'.

DEIRDRE: *(Laughing)* No, you didn't.

MONICA: No, I didn't. But I'm not so sure my song and dance about the wonders of modern medicine did much to reassure her. The kid's not stupid.

DEIRDRE: I've thought about it. You know, what I would do if I got it. You're the only one I could depend on. You'd take care of me, wouldn't you, Monica?

MONICA: *(Approaches, DEIRDRE)* Of course I would. I'd sell everything I have and buy a little cottage on the lake. You'd come and live with me and I'd take you swimming every single day.

DEIRDRE: But I can't swim.

MONICA : I know, honey.

DEIRDRE: And what about you? What if you do get it?

MONICA : Steve's got that all figured out. He says we'll take up skydiving together.

DEIRDRE: Skydiving? What good will that do?

MONICA: Well at first we'll just be another retired couple enjoying a hobby together, but he figures eventually, I'm bound to forget what that ripcord is for.

DEIRDRE: Oh, Monica, I could never face this without you.

MONICA: It's the right thing to do, De. We have to think of mother and her dignity. As embarrassed as you and Dan were last night, imagine what she would think if she knew.

DEIRDRE: Oh God, you're right. She'd die a thousand deaths, as she would say.

MONICA: We can't protect her from the disease, Deirdre, but we have to do more to shield her from the indignity that comes with it. At least as far as the family is concerned.

DEIRDRE: You're right. I agree.

MONICA: To placing her?

DEIRDRE: Yes.

MONICA: Good then. I've got some recommendations for a few places. We can go look at them next week, if you like.

DEIRDRE: Okay, let's do that.
(She grabs one of the tissues from the table and wipes her eyes)

MONICA: Why don't you get out of here for a while? Go on downtown. *(Looks at her watch)* It's almost lunchtime. You can go to the office and seduce your husband, and then have a go at it on top of his desk. No bouncing required.

DEIRDRE: You don't mind?

MONICA: No, I'll stay with her. I want to ask her how her night was.

DEIRDRE: You're impossible, but thanks. *(Jumps up, goes to coat rack)* I'll try not to be too long.

MONICA: *(Waves her off)* Just enjoy it.

DEIRDRE: *(Puts on coat)* See if you can get her to eat some of that applesauce, will you? She hasn't eaten a thing all day.

MONICA: Okay. But before you go, I have just one question about last night.

DEIRDRE: What is it?

MONICA: Do you always make love with the dog in the room? I find --that kind of creepy. *(She shivers)*
--Ooh,
(To MOTHER)
--Don't you think that's kind of creepy?

(MOTHER smiles and nods)

DEIRDRE: Good-bye, Monica.

(Exit DEIRDRE)

MONICA: I think that went rather well, don't you?

(MOTHER hums softly, as she folds her napkins. MONICA moves her chair closer to MOTHER. She gently takes her mother by the chin and turns her head so their eyes meet)

MONICA: Hello, Mom.

MOTHER: Hello.

MONICA: It's me, Monica.

MOTHER: Oh, yes.
(She turns her head away and resumes her folding)

(Beat)

MONICA: You need to eat something, Mom. Let's see what we have here.
(She takes the cover off the applesauce)
This applesauce is homemade! Where in the hell does she find time to make homemade applesauce?
(She tastes it)
Oh, that's good. It's your recipe, Mom. Here, try some.
(She spoons some applesauce towards her mother's mouth but MOTHER gently pushes her hand away)

(MONICA eats the spoon of applesauce herself)

MONICA: This is delicious. Do you remember when you taught us how to make applesauce? We picked the whole bushel of apples ourselves and then we spent that afternoon baking pies and making applesauce. You, me and Deirdre. Do you remember?

(*MOTHER hums and folds*)

MONICA: C'mon. Try some.

(*She spoons the applesauce to MOTHER's mouth. MOTHER pushes at the spoon violently, sending it flying into the air*)

(*Beat*)

MONICA: Okay, so you don't want applesauce.

(*She runs her hand gently across her mother's temple, brushing back her hair*)
Maybe you know better than all the rest of us. Why keep feeding a body that has so cruelly betrayed you? Makes you wonder who's the crazy one...

(*She spends a few seconds stroking her mother's hair. Then with slow, deliberate movements she takes another spoon, and then a spoonful of applesauce, spoons it to her mouth, and leans back in the chair savoring the flavor.*)

MONICA: That day you taught us to make applesauce, how long ago was that? I can remember it so clearly...and yet, I can't remember the last time you said my name.

(*She leans forward with her head in her hands*)

(*Beat*)

(*MOTHER picks up a spoon and puts it in the applesauce. She takes a spoonful, stares at it a moment. She lifts the spoon in the air sways it gently side to side. She begins to hum, a droning sound like an airplane. MONICA hearing the droning sound sits up as MOTHER drives the spoon towards her and into her startled, open mouth. She swallows the applesauce as MOTHER places the spoon back in the bowl. MOTHER takes one*) *of the folded napkins and wipes at* MONICA'S *mouth. Dropping the napkin, she reaches out and gently strokes* MONICA'S *cheek.)*

MOTHER : That's...my girl.

*(*MONICA *holds her mother's hand against her cheek)*

(Lights Fade)

THE END

The Key

by Vivian Neuwirth

Produced by manhattan**theatre**source *in Group A of EstroGenius 2012 with the following cast and crew:*

Director: Kathleen O'Neill

Anne: Kayla Wickes

Davi: Alex Kliment

Sound Designer: Amber Gallery

Lighting Designer: Kayla Goble

Stage Manager: Katt Masterson

Costume Designer: Julija Frodina

CONTACT
vivianneuwirth@gmail.com

CHARACTERS

ANNE – Late 20s-early30s. Young Urban Professional. Dressed in a stylish suit. Stunningly beautiful. Striking contrast of blond hair and dark eyes. Has an unusual combination of sexual appeal and innocence.

DAVI – 30s. Israeli soldier on leave. Wears jeans, shirt and jacket. Extremely good looking, Israeli accent. Has a military bearing and an air of command. Strong sexual appeal. There is nothing innocent about him.

Time: The middle of the night. September. Not too long ago.

Setting: A small apartment on the top floor of a brownstone in Greenwich Village. Decorated in the style of a country cottage, Americana. There is a window, a small couch with a throw folded over it, some chairs, little tables, a fireplace and a log holder containing logs. Offstage are a kitchen, bedroom and bathroom.

IN BLACK: We hear laughter which gets louder as ANNE *and* DAVI *come up the stairs. They burst into* ANNE'S *apartment laughing uproariously. They have been drinking. For a moment they stand in the dark catching their breath. Then* ANNE *turns on the light. They look at each other. There is an obvious sexual attraction between them. The power of the attraction should be like a third character in the play, appearing insistently, especially during the silences and pauses.*

DAVI *looks around. He has a Nikon camera around his neck.* ANNE *watches him.*

DAVI: This is great.

ANNE: Thank you.

ANNE *discreetly turns over framed photo on mantelpiece.* DAVI *observes her.*

DAVI: You have a fireplace.

ANNE: Yes.

DAVI: *(starts to put logs in fireplace)* Let's make a fire.

ANNE: *(stops him, their hands touch)* It's already very warm in here. Don't you feel warm -?

DAVI: I have never seen a fireplace before. We don't have them in Israel -

ANNE: *(removing her jacket)* I have southern exposure.

DAVI: Exposure?

ANNE: The sun. I'm on the top floor so it hits the roof and comes in through the windows. It makes the room hot. Too hot for a fire.

DAVI: *(aiming his camera at her and the fireplace)* It would make a great picture -

ANNE: It's nice in the winter. When it's snowing. For the holidays -

DAVI: *(taking a picture)* To remember you.

Their eyes meet. A pause.

DAVI: *(replacing lens cap and putting camera on table)* So, this is what you call a walk up?

ANNE: Yes. A walk-up in a brownstone.

DAVI: A brown stone?

ANNE: It's not really brown. It can be any color. Well, not any color. It's landmarked.

DAVI: Land marked?

ANNE: It's a historic district. Actually, the Meatpacking District.

DAVI: I don't understand.

ANNE: Slaughterhouses. Where they butcher meat.

DAVI: This is historic?

ANNE: Uh... it's called the Far West Village. Very far from the subway but near the river.

DAVI: That is something I would like to see -

ANNE: I'll take you -

DAVI: Before I leave.

A beat.

DAVI: Thank you for inviting me, Anne.

ANNE: Thank you for walking me home.

Pause.

DAVI: Is this all yours?

ANNE: What do you mean?

DAVI: No other people live here?

ANNE: *(beat)* Oh. You mean a roommate? No.

DAVI: *(glancing at turned over photo)* No boyfriend?

ANNE: *(beat)* No.

DAVI: Why?

ANNE: Well, of course, I've had boyfriends. But...

DAVI: *(moving closer to her)* But?

ANNE: What about you? Do you have a girlfriend? In Israel?

DAVI: Not right now.

He kisses her. She pulls away.

ANNE: Please. Don't.

DAVI: I apologize.

ANNE: I don't usually bring strangers home like this -

DAVI: I am not a stranger. I am Chaim's best friend. We were properly introduced. We had dinner. We -

ANNE: Of course you're not a stranger - I didn't mean -

DAVI: You are friends. You and Debbie -

ANNE: Best friends. Since college. Where did you meet Chaim?

DAVI: IDF.

ANNE: IDF?

DAVI: Israeli Defense Force.
  (silence) The army.

ANNE: Is that like the reserves?

DAVI: For Chaim it is the reserves. For me - life.

ANNE: Oh.
  (beat)
  Somehow I can't see Chaim as a soldier.

DAVI: He might surprise you.
  (after a pause) They are a strange couple.

ANNE: I don't think so. It was love at first sight.

DAVI: For her.

(beat)

She is not Jewish. Is she?

ANNE: She's converting.

DAVI: She is?

ANNE: Have you met his mother?

They laugh.

DAVI: She would do this for him?

ANNE: I think she would do anything for him. Follow him anywhere.

DAVI: To Israel?

ANNE: Anywhere.

They sit on couch staring at fireplace. His hand rests on her knee.

ANNE: Have you enjoyed your visit to New York, Davi?

DAVI: Oh yes. Debbie and Chaim took me everywhere.

ANNE: What did you see?

DAVI: All the famous places. The United Nations, The Intrepid, Central Park, Times Square –

ANNE: Did you see a Broadway show?

DAVI tucks a strand of hair which has fallen in her eyes behind her ear.

ANNE: *(cont'd)* Davi, what else did you see?

DAVI: The Yankee Stadium. I saw the Yankees. They beat the Red Sox.

ANNE: You like baseball?

DAVI: I like soccer. But in New York I like baseball. In New York I like everything.

ANNE: What did you like the most?

DAVI: *(caressing her neck)* Meeting you.

ANNE: *(rising, moving away)* Would you like to see The White Horse?

DAVI: White horse?

ANNE: It's a tavern right around the corner. It's very famous. They say it's where Dylan Thomas drank himself to death.
(silence)
Dylan Thomas. The poet?

DAVI: I know who Dylan Thomas is.

ANNE picks up DAVI'S camera gingerly and aims it at him.

ANNE: It's open all night. You can take a picture. If you're not too tired –

DAVI: The lens cap... it's on...

ANNE: *(flustered, trying to remove lens cap)* Oh, the...yes...

DAVI crosses to her and slowly takes camera away, putting it on table.

DAVI: I am not at all tired. I am wide-awake.

He kisses her again. She gives in, then pushes him away.

DAVI: Why did you invite me to your apartment?

ANNE: I wanted to show you the Village.

DAVI: It could have ended at the door.
(beat)
You brought me into your home. You live alone, yes?

ANNE: Yes.

DAVI: Why pretend? *(pause)* When you came into the restaurant I saw it in your eyes -

ANNE: I was just surprised. When you stood up. Who does that anymore -?

DAVI: I've seen that look before –

ANNE: What -?

DAVI: The look of surrender.

They stare at each other.

ANNE: I didn't offer you anything.
  (after a pause, moves past him to kitchen)
  Would you like something to drink?

DAVI: I have had enough to drink.

ANNE: *(offstage)* I have Pellegrino. *(silence)* Sparkling water. Would
  you like that?

DAVI: Yes. Please. After that meal.

ANNE: *(offstage)* Didn't you like the restaurant? It was my idea –
  Middle Eastern food. I thought you would feel more at home.

DAVI: It was Arabic.

ANNE *returns with two little bottles of Pellegrino. She offers him one.*

ANNE: Oh. Sorry. Next time -

DAVI: I am leaving tomorrow, Anne.

Pause. ANNE *puts her bottle down on table, slowly walks to* DAVI *and
gently kisses him. He responds with a prolonged kiss. They become fiercely
impassioned.*

DAVI: You smell wonderful. Your hair, your skin. *(unbuttons her
  blouse)* You are so beautiful -

He sees an old-fashioned key hanging on a chain around her neck.

DAVI: *(teasing her)* What does this key open?

They laugh.

ANNE: *(unbuttons his shirt, sees large scar on his chest)*
  My god. How did you get that scar? What happened to you?

DAVI: The war.

ANNE: *(a moment)* I'm sorry.

DAVI: It is nothing.

ANNE: *(touching his chest)* Nothing?

DAVI: I am alive.

ANNE: Where did you fight?

He tries to stop her mouth with kisses.

ANNE: *(cont'd)* You fought Palestinians -?

DAVI: Ssshh... don't talk about them now -

ANNE: They did this to you -?

DAVI: They are animals.

ANNE: Did you kill anyone?
(silence)
How many Palestinians did you kill?

DAVI: As many as I could! Why are you asking this?

ANNE: *(pause, turning away)* I'm Palestinian.

DAVI: *(he freezes)* What?

ANNE: My parents were born in Bethlehem. In Palestine.

DAVI: You have blond hair.

ANNE: We're Christian.

DAVI: That makes it okay, then? That is different?

ANNE: Is it?

DAVI: *(buttoning his shirt)* Lo nakhon... This is a joke. A bad joke.

ANNE: *(covering herself)* I don't know why I told you. I don't like to
tell anyone.

He holds her face between his hands and looks at her.

DAVI: I don't believe you. Say something in Arabic.

ANNE: All I know is a song my Aunt Jehad taught me.

DAVI: Jihad?! Her name is Jihad?!

ANNE: Yes.

DAVI: You know what that means -?

ANNE: It's not what you think -

DAVI: It means you are my enemy -

ANNE: This is why I didn't want to tell you -

DAVI: Sing it.

ANNE: I don't remember -

DAVI: *(pushing her)* You are lying -

ANNE: I don't want to remember!

DAVI: *(pushing her again)* Sing the fucking song!

Faltering at first, she softly sings a tender Arabic lullaby. She clutches the key on the chain around her neck, which emboldens her. Her eyes fill with tears.

ANNE:
  Yalla tnaam, Yalla tnaam
  Ledbahla taayr el hamaam
  Ruh ya hamaan la tsaddi'
  Bedhak `a Nina la tnaam
  Nina, Nina el handa'a
  Sha`arek aswad wa mna'a
  Willi habba biboosa
  Willi ma habba shoo byetla'a

A long pause.

DAVI: Do Debbie and Chaim know?

ANNE: Only Debbie.
  (beat)
  Tonight when she said good-night she warned me to be careful. I
  thought she meant to be careful being alone with you.
  (pause)
  Are you going to tell Chaim?

DAVI: You want me to lie for you? To lie to my best friend? I will not
  lie for you Anne.

ANNE: I'm afraid he'll hate me.

DAVI: Hate is a very strong word.

ANNE: Not when it comes to Palestine.

DAVI: There is no such thing as Palestine.

ANNE: *(wistfully)* Someday -

DAVI: Shut up! What do you know? You know nothing! Have you even been there?

ANNE: Someday I'll go... to Palestine.

DAVI: Never! That will never happen! You understand nothing. You only see from a distance. I live inside, always looking over my shoulder.
(grabbing her) Looking for people like -*(he stops himself)*

ANNE: Say it. People like me.
(silence)
You hate me.

DAVI: *(pause)* I am trying to hate you.

ANNE: You want to leave now, don't you? Go ahead. Leave.

DAVI: *(heading towards door)* I should leave.
(hesitating) But there is nowhere else I want to be.
(turning back)
God, what have you done to me? What is happening here?

ANNE: Peace?

DAVI: Truce.

After a moment, he goes to mantelpiece. Picks up photo.

DAVI: Tell me. What other secrets are you hiding?

She tries to take photo from him. He resists. It falls on floor and breaks.

ANNE: *(quietly, holding back tears)* My family...

DAVI: *(picking up photo)* It is just a crack. I can fix it.

ANNE: Our house in Bethlehem...

DAVI: It is very grand.

ANNE: Grandpapa was the mayor.

DAVI: Really. The mayor.

ANNE: Really. Then Jordanian Ambassador. My mother grew up
with the Prince's children. She was invited to tea at the Royal
Palace. A chauffeur would pick her up after school.
(touching picture)
See her dress? She loved everything French. Her clothes were
from Paris.

DAVI: She is a very beautiful woman.

ANNE: Was.

DAVI: *(offers her Pellegrino)* I am sorry.

ANNE: One day my father came to court her and took her away. To
America. Grandpapa didn't want to part with her. But he knew
what was coming so he let her go. They got out just in time. The
tanks entered Bethlehem a few days later.

A pause.

DAVI: So you were born here?

ANNE: I was the child that made them American.
(pause)
But we were different. I didn't know we were different until my
birthday party. I was five. Daddy got balloons and Mama
prepared American food. We waited for the guests who never
came. We waited all day. After it got dark, Mama took a pin and
popped the balloons one by one. She said, "*Habibi,* if anyone asks
you just say we're French."
(beat)
That's when I started lying.

A pause.

DAVI: And your father?

ANNE: He promised her everything but all he ever had was a dream. in his dream we spoke only English.

A long pause.

ANNE *carefully puts photo on mantelpiece.*

ANNE: This is the last picture of them all together. It's fading...
(*pause*)
She never saw her family again. After the partition, after - after the borders were drawn, they were never allowed to go back. All she had was this.
(*touching the key*)
The key to the house. Now it's mine. She made me promise that someday I would claim it.

DAVI: You live in the past. That key opens nothing. Forget it. That was a long time ago.

ANNE: It still belongs to us.

DAVI: You know only one side of the story.

ANNE: I know my mother had a broken heart. She knew she would never go home again.

DAVI: That is war.

ANNE: What about my family? Where are they now? Why should they make that sacrifice?

DAVI: Sacrifice? I had a sister. One day she was walking to a shop to buy perfume. That is all. But she was walking in the wrong place. Any place can be the wrong place and that day the wrong place was where she was walking. The explosion took my sister and the only thing left of her was the scent of her perfume in her room in the house that is OUR house in Jerusalem!
(*sobbing*)
Sacrifice?! You don't know what it feels like!

ANNE: (*quietly*) I know what shame feels like. Shame with every bombing. Shame to say my name. My name isn't Anne. It's... Aida. It means, "I am returning".

DAVI: Even your name is a lie?! Who are you?!

ANNE: *(crying)* I don't know! I've lied all my life! But here - no one knows my name. I can belong. I can be anyone. I have the perfect job. The perfect apartment. Aida's just a memory. A feeling that I have of something... missing. I know I should want to find her but Anne is. Anne is...

DAVI: *(buttoning her blouse)* There is nothing missing. You are Aida. You don't have to lie anymore.

A guitar version of the lullaby begins to play. DAVI *gets the throw from the couch and places it in front of the fireplace. They lie down side by side. After a moment,* ANNE *drifts into sleep.* DAVI *removes his jacket and covers her with it. He watches her, stroking her hair. He falls asleep. Music plays until lights change to dawn.* ANNE *wakes first. She sits up, gazing at* DAVI *sleeping. He wakes.*

DAVI: Aida...let's make a fire.

ANNE: I have to get ready for work now.

DAVI: Not now. Not until morning.

Sunrise breaks through curtains.

ANNE: It is morning.

DAVI: So soon? I am leaving tonight.

ANNE: Cancel your flight.

DAVI: Cancel?

ANNE: Yes.

DAVI: And then what? Aida? Then what?

ANNE: *(pause)* Then "the lovers lie abed with all their griefs in their arms."

DAVI: What?

ANNE: Dylan Thomas. The -

DAVI: *(laughing)* I know who Dylan Thomas is.

ANNE: "Not for the proud man apart...
  (trying to remember)
  Nor for the towering dead,
  But for the lovers,
  Their arms round the griefs of the ages."

DAVI: Before I can be your grief I have to be your lover.

ANNE: Cancel your flight!

DAVI: You are asking me to desert?! This I cannot do.

ANNE gets up angrily and goes into the bathroom.

DAVI: I will go with you to work.

ANNE: *(offstage)* No!
  (pause)
  Yes. You can meet me for lunch. There's a restaurant where I work. It's famous.

DAVI: When?

ANNE: *(offstage)* 1 o'clock.

DAVI stands, tucks shirt into pants.

DAVI: Where? Where shall I meet you?

ANNE comes out of the bathroom. She opens curtains. Sunlight streams in.

ANNE: There.

DAVI: The World Trade Center? That is where you work?

ANNE: You can walk along the river. All the way down to Battery Park. You can see the Statue of Liberty. Especially on a day like today. In September the air is so clear.

DAVI: We can walk together. You promised to show me the river.

ANNE: We can go tonight. At sunset.

DAVI: No. *(putting his arms around her)* Don't go to work today.

ANNE: *(breaking away, going into bedroom)* Let me go. I don't like to be late.

DAVI: *(taking out his cell phone)* Wait! Give me your mobile number

ANNE: *(offstage)* I'll give it to you later.

DAVI: Then take mine.

ANNE: *(offstage)* We have time for all that. Later -

DAVI: How will we meet? Where will I go?

ANNE comes out of bedroom wearing a different top. Heads towards door, grabbing her purse.

ANNE: I'll meet you in the restaurant. At the top of One. Tower One. Bring your camera.

DAVI: That is it? Lunch and then good-bye? Why must you go -?

ANNE: Why should I stay? For a few hours? Something to regret?

DAVI: You know it is not like that. This is different.

ANNE: *(at door, hand on doorknob)* Davi, please. Please be there at one.

DAVI: Don't go. *Habibi. Willi habba biboosa -*

She stops and turns to him.

ANNE: What?

DAVI: Don't go.

ANNE: No, the other part.

DAVI: *Habibi -*

ANNE: You know Arabic?

DAVI: I know enough. *(with outstretched arms)* I will teach you Arabic.

She walks slowly towards him.

DAVI: *Muftaah.*

ANNE: *Muftaah...*
    (beat)
    What does it mean?

DAVI: It means key.

She drops her bag on the floor. They embrace. Lights through window very bright. Slow fade on them as lights up brighter and brighter through window.

BLACKOUT

THE END

Acknowledgments:

"In My Craft or Sullen Art" by Dylan Thomas (Public Domain)

"Yalla Tnam" Traditional (Public Domain)
Recording available at :
http://www.youtube.com/watch?v=GinP_ZRgAoY
Sheet music available on request.

"Yalla Tnam" for solo guitar arranged and performed by Alex Kliment. Recording available on request.

Buying the Farm

by Lezlie Revelle

Produced by manhattantheatresource *in Group A of EstroGenius 2012 with the following cast and crew:*

Director: Audrey Alford

Vivian: Sue Ellen Mandell

Gladys: Laurel Lockhart*

Myrna: Nancy Evans

Ruth: Limor Hakim*

Sound Designer: Amber Gallery

Lighting Designer: Kayla Goble

Stage Manager: Katt Masterson

Costume Designer: Julija Frodina

*Member of Actors' Equity Association

CONTACT
lezlie@lezlierevelle.com

CHARACTERS

VIVIAN-60s+ Ringleader, mostly serious with a good head on her shoulders. She is kind and thoughtful, but means business. The play opens with VIVIAN changing from stylish clothes into frumpy old-lady clothes. She may add a wig for emphasis.

MYRNA-60s+ Smartass. She's hard, sassy and saucy. MYRNA changes/adds her old-lady clothes near the end of the scene

GLADYS-60s+ Deceptively soft and airy. Sharp as a tack with a surprising hard edge when needed. She arrives in her old-lady clothes, talking on a cell phone and carrying a cane that she can wield like a short quarter-staff.

RUTH –late 20s Reporter. Was contacted by VIVIAN to do a human interest piece on women aging in America. She has a questionable deal with her paper, but despite that and her brush with the questionable legality of her writing, she is not yet a cynic.

Time: the present.

Place: A simply furnished apartment. Couch, one or two chairs, coffee table, and a mirrored bureau.

(LIGHTS UP on apartment. There is a couch and coffee table CS. RUTH sits in chair SL of couch. She is taking notes as she listens. VIVIAN stands at mirrored bureau SR, dressing. We are joining a conversation in progress)

VIVIAN: There was nothing gradual about it. It just... happened. One day everything was as it always has been. And the next I was . . . invisible.

RUTH: That sounds a bit exaggerated.

VIVIAN: I wish it were. It was truly as if suddenly and inexplicably, over half the people in my known universe no longer saw me. Wait staff glided by me, people nudged me out of line. . .

RUTH: How is that possible?

VIVIAN: *(gives RUTH a piercing look)* You tell me.

(When RUTH has no answer, VIVIAN continues)

VIVIAN: *(cont'd)* It only took a few weeks of this for me to start to feel crazy. I tried to be more noticeable – I wore what I saw as more fashionable clothes and hair, more makeup. . .

(MYRNA enters carrying a tray of tea or lemonade)

MYRNA: And merely ended up looking like an old whore.

VIVIAN: Look who's talking

(MYRNA makes a Myrna Loy face at VIVIAN)

VIVIAN: *(cont'd)* I may have gone overboard. . . . This is Myrna.

MYRNA: Hello there.

RUTH: Myrna? That's an unusual name.

MYRNA: I was named after Myrna Loy. Do you know. . .?

(RUTH shakes her head)

MYRNA: *(cont'd)* Of course not. Find a DVD of "The Thin Man ", honey. Watch it. Trust me. *(undertone)* It'll do you good.

(VIVIAN clears her throat)

MYRNA: *(cont'd) (innocently)* Oh, I'm sorry. Were you in the middle of something?

 (MYRNA smiles sweetly and VIVIAN gives her a look)

VIVIAN: *(to RUTH)* Where were we, dear?

(RUTH looks back over her notes)

RUTH: Makeup and fashion.

MYRNA: Ah, yes. Tramp du jour.

VIVIAN: As I was saying. I may have gone overboard. Regardless, this all – the clothes, the hair, the makeup – had the antithetical effect to what I'd hoped. Now I was invisible only to some. To the rest, I was something to be forcibly ignored.

MYRNA: And can you blame them?

RUTH: Was it really that bad?

MYRNA: Honey, let me tell you —

RUTH: *(a bit exasperated)* I mean the ignoring. —

VIVIAN: Ladies, we are on a timetable. If you don't let me finish --

(GLADYS enters, talking on a cell phone)

GLADYS: *(into phone)* No dear. You have to press the alt key, then you can see the menu bar. . . .*(waves to the others)* No that's the menu bar that will let you access compatibility settings. Mm. . . Yes –Yes, dear. . . .Right. Then you can see if you have a backwards compatibility. . . .Okay. Bye-bye now. *(shakes her head as she hangs up)*Young people. Helpless.

RUTH: *(gives a little laugh and shakes her head before echoing)* Young people.

GLADYS: *(takes in the scene)* What, no cookies? *(to RUTH)* I'm sorry, dear. They're not used to entertaining.

(RUTH can't seem to find an appropriate response)

GLADYS: *(cont'd)* You're Ruth?

RUTH: Yes. . . . Yes. Pleased to meet you.

GLADYS: Well, aren't you sweet. I'm Gladys. You're writing the article?

RUTH: Well, I —

VIVIAN: I'm sure you'd find it all more interesting if these old bats would let me talk.

(Looks sternly at the older women)

VIVIAN: *(cont'd)* Thank you. I was in a grim place, Ruth. I woke up one morning, teetering between depression and dipping my toe into waters that might lead to bat-shit-crazy.

(GLADYS and MYRNA make eye contact and snort/giggle. VIVIAN throws a brush at MYRNA)

MYRNA: What? I'm hanging on every word!

(VIVIAN throws something else at MYRNA)

MYRNA; *(cont'd)* She was laughing too!

GLADYS: Go on, Viv.

VIVIAN: I washed my face in cold water to try and shake the malaise that had descended upon me.

(RUTH stares at VIVIAN, glances at the others)

GLADYS: She always talks like that, dear.

MYRNA: Always has.

VIVIAN: I was a mess. I hadn't showered, dressed, or left the house in days. It wasn't pretty.

MYRNA: You're telling me.

GLADYS: It was rather frightening, actually. I want you know that, Ruth. All joking aside, frightening.

VIVIAN: I gazed into the mirror to ask myself yet again what was happening. And it hit me. I was old.

MYRNA: Boy howdy.

VIVIAN: Shut up, Myr.

GLADYS: We're all old. And we're going to die of natural causes if you don't get on with it. And if you don't let her.

VIVIAN: Thank you Gladys. . . . Where was I?

MYRNA: You were old.

VIVIAN: Right. But not old enough to be interesting. Not old enough to need help or garner pity. Just. . . Old. I fought it. Aggressive skin care, different hairstyles yet again, different makeup. . . But when you're old, sister, you're old.

MYRNA: Don't let those Covergirl ads fool you.

GLADYS: You're just old.

MYRNA: You can take that to the bank.

VIVIAN: And I plan to.

RUTH: What do you mean?

GLADYS: Not quite yet.

MYRNA: We all went through it. What Vivian is talking about. Or at least versions of it.

GLADYS: I got very good at needing help. *(fumbles with something)* Oh, dear!

(RUTH jumps up to help her. GLADYS becomes completely calm and cool and in control again)

GLADYS: *(cont'd)* See?

RUTH: But surely you don't need to pretend to be helpless or dotty to get attention.

MYRNA: So young.

VIVIAN: Darling, I wish we were telling you tales. I became an accomplished nursing home infiltrator.

RUTH: Why on earth would you have to infiltrate a nursing home?

MYRNA: I think the question you mean is, why would you want to?

VIVIAN: For the company. I pretended to live there.

RUTH: But those places are awful! No one ever visits those old peo— I mean the . . . the uh . . .

MYRNA: I think the word you're looking for is inmates.

GLADYS: Residents. You're so dramatic.

RUTH: Still. Surely they knew you didn't belong.

MYRNA: Out of the mouths of babes.

VIVIAN: I snuck in at night and made up stories to entertain the night shift. They are odd ducks as well; lonely in their own way. Often happy with that, but open to the strange companionship of a lonely old woman.

RUTH: That's just . . . Awful. *(to MYRNA)* What was your thing?

MYRNA: *(snorts)* I was just that cranky old hag. Bitchiness always suited me better than dottiness or yarn-spinning.

RUTH: And now?

GLADYS: Well now we're going to do something about it, dear.

VIVIAN: And that's why you're here.

GLADYS: To tell the story.

RUTH: I suppose it could make a good Op Ed series. Certainly tragic enough. My gran raised me. I owe pretty much all I am to her.

I'm glad she hasn't had to deal with any of this.

VIVIAN: Hasn't she?

RUTH: Of course not. She has me.

VIVIAN: Hm.

MYRNA: You may as well finish it out.

GLADYS: *(glancing at her watch)* Yes, it's nearly time.

VIVIAN: Yes, I suppose it is. There is a bit more to the story.

RUTH: Okay...

VIVIAN: Today we are going to rob a bank.

RUTH: You're going to . . . what?

GLADYS: Rob a bank, dear.

MYRNA: Buy the farm, as it were.

VIVIAN: We're going to change the world for women like us.

GLADYS: We really are going to buy a farm. Isn't it wonderful?

RUTH: You're joking.

MYRNA: We're dead serious.

VIVIAN: It'll be like an artist's colony. Only you don't have to be an artist to live there. You only have to be old.

MYRNA: We're not helpless, you know.

GLADYS: But we are quite crafty. Which is why we'll succeed. . . . And, come to think about it, how we'll support ourselves.

MYRNA: Gladys.

GLADYS: Get it, dear? Crafty *(points to head)* and crafty *(holds up a doily or something)!*

RUTH: I get it. I just don't get why you're telling me.

GLADYS: So you can let others know, dear.

MYRNA: Yes. You'll be our . . . what's the word? Go-between.

VIVIAN: Your story will get the word out, then interested oldsters can contact you to find us.

RUTH: You can't be serious.

GLADYS: Of course we are, dear. You're writing is wonderful.

RUTH: That's not what I mean —

GLADYS: And never you mind about that little snafu with the academic dishonesty.

RUTH: I mean how — What? How . . . how do you know about that?

MYRNA: They covered that right up, didn't they?

RUTH: But. . . but . . . That's classified!

GLADYS: You're telling me! It wasn't so much behind a firewall as a fire fortress!

RUTH: But how . . You. . . But you're . . .

GLADYS: You know, that's just what they said about me over at that junior college.

MYRNA: Always underestimating us.

RUTH: *(weakly)* But. . .

MYRNA: Honestly. Are we sure we want this girl representing us?

RUTH: This is insane.

VIVIAN: Think . . . eccentric.

RUTH: *(considers a moment)* This is ridiculous. *(gathers her things and heads to door)* How could you possibly believe I'd buy this story?

VIVIAN: Oh, we're telling the truth.

RUTH: Fine. Then what made you think I'd be a part of it? *(turns to go)*

GLADYS: *(texting as she speaks)* Oh, I don't think you want to do that, dear.

RUTH: I can't let you get away with this.

MYRNA: You may want to reconsider that.

RUTH: Why on earth would I?

GLADYS: The romance of secret interviews?

MYRNA: Maybe they'll call you "old throat."

(GLADYS throws her doily at MYRNA)

MYRNA: *(cont'd)* Or maybe because you know that we know about that little academic cover-up. . .

VIVIAN: But if none of that is enough. . .

(landline rings)

VIVIAN: *(cont'd)* Ah, D'Artagnan.

MYRNA: Answer it for God's sake.

(GLADYS picks up the phone but holds it directly out to RUTH)

GLADYS: It's for you, dear.

RUTH: What? Who . . . *(takes phone reluctantly)* Hello? . . . Grandma?? *(RUTH listens, then hands the phone back to GLADYS without saying a word. GLADYS hangs up phone, and looks concernedly at RUTH)*

GLADYS: Are you okay, dear?

RUTH: That was my gran.

GLADYS: Yes, dear.

RUTH: She's part of this?

MYRNA: She's quick.

VIVIAN: She's the fourth member of our team.

RUTH: But . . . This is insane. I need to think. . . . I need a drink. . . . I need to sit down.

(RUTH sits. GLADYS refills her glass)

GLADYS: Probably not as strong as you'd like.

MYRNA: There's whisky in the kitchen.

VIVIAN: Not now, Myrna.

(*VIVIAN watches RUTH closely*)

RUTH: She knew? Gran knew about. . . about my . . .

VIVIAN: About your little journalistic deal with the devil? Yes.

RUTH: But she never said a thing.

MYRNA: And you're surprised?

RUTH: I was sure she'd disown me. I couldn't bear the thought of letting her down.

MYRNA: See what I mean? Always underestimating.

(*MYRNA begins to costume up, donning wig and clothes that make her look older than she is*)

RUTH: What's her part in all this?

VIVIAN: Driver. Gladys and I will be taking care of the bank. We do dotty better. Myrna here is going to have a little "heart attack" a few doors down. Delores – your grandmother – will be driving the ambulance. Though, granted, she doesn't look very convincing.

MYRNA: Not to mention she's a dead awful driver.

VIVIAN: (*shrug*) But it's what we've got to work with.

RUTH: I'll do it.

GLADYS: Do what, dear?

MYRNA: Honestly, Gladys. Write the article. Be the contact.

RUTH: No. Well, yes. Probably. But what I meant was, I'll drive the ambulance.

VIVIAN: I'm afraid that's out of the question. You don't know anything about the plan.

RUTH: I know enough. You tell me where and when to show up and

I'll drive you batty dames wherever you want to go. Just let me do this. It's too dangerous. . . . That's my price.

(*MYRNA makes a move and looks like she's about to say something, but VIVIAN stills her with a hand*)

VIVIAN: You're sure?

RUTH: Try me.

VIVIAN: Very well. You'll need these.

(*VIVIAN hands RUTH a folder and cell phone from a bureau drawer*)

VIVIAN: *(cont'd)* The details are in there. That's a disposable phone. We'll call you on that if anything changes.

(*RUTH stares at the items in her hands, then gathers her things and walks toward the door. She stops and turns back*)

RUTH: How on earth are you going to handle security guards? Or younger, fitter people?

(*VIVIAN takes a walker from the corner whose legs appeared to be wrapped with wire. She aims the feet at RUTH and nods to the feet*)

VIVIAN: Tasers.

(*GLADYS stands and impressively wields a cane like a small quarterstaff*)

GLADYS: I like our chances.

(*RUTH gapes at GLADYS*)

GLADYS *(cont'd)* Stage combat classes.

MYRNA: God bless the junior college.

(*RUTH stares at them each a moment longer*)

RUTH: Insane.

(*RUTH exits*)

GLADYS: How did she know? How did Delores know she would do that?

MYRNA: *(continues costuming up)* Honestly, Gladys. Have you never watched a caper movie? I'm the sexy, witty one, you're the sweet, awkward technology expert, Viv here is the master planner, and Delores is the people person.

VIVIAN: *(snorts)* Come on, Gladys. You know as well as I do that when you've been alive as long as we have, you just know things.

GLADYS: I suppose so.

VIVIAN: Come on, ladies. Let's see it.

(GLADYS seem to shrink and ad libs in a dotty old voice while MYRNA clutches at her chest and arm, wheezing and appearing to be in pain)

VIVIAN: Lovely. Let's go buy that farm.

BLACKOUT

THE END

Jumping In

by Seth Freeman

Produced by manhattan**theatre**source *in Group A of EstroGenius 2012 with the following cast and crew:*

Director: T Valada-Viars

Junie: Justine Hall

Puma: Helen Barnes

Sound Designer: Amber Gallery

Lighting Designer: Kayla Goble

Stage Manager: Katt Masterson

Costume Designer: Julija Frodina

CONTACT
seth.o.freeman@gmail.com

CHARACTERS

JUNIE – late 20's -40's, a school teacher

PUMA – about 18, a poor student.

Setting: A public school classroom.

A class room in a public high school. There's a blackboard or white board, desk, and -- only if possible, some shelves, posters on the wall, florescent lights, worn blinds. JUNIE, the teacher who uses this room, is in a desk chair, at some remove from the desk. A young woman of high school age, PUMA, full of attitude, dressed in baggy everything, is tying JUNIE to the chair with phone wire.

JUNIE: Hey, easy.

PUMA: I ain't hurting you.

JUNIE: This chair is kind of fragile.

PUMA: *(removing a spray can from a scruffy pack)* I ain't messin' with the chair.

She spray paints the words "FUCK SKOL," on the board, steps back to review her work.

JUNIE: "Fuck Skol"? You're against chewing tobacco?

PUMA: Fuck school. School. I hate school, bitch. That's why I didn't want to come here. I don't even like being around a school.

JUNIE: Duh.

PUMA: *(wheeling on JUNIE menacingly)* Hey!

JUNIE: Hey. It's kind of obvious you haven't spent much time in a class room.

PUMA: Are you a teacher or something?

JUNIE: This is my room. I'm a teacher.

PUMA: What the fuck you doin' here this time of night anyway?

JUNIE: Lesson plans.

PUMA: What?

JUNIE: We actually plan what and how we're going to teach.

PUMA: You mean, like, you're working? This late? That's loco, girl.

JUNIE: You're probably right.

PUMA: Nobody was supposed to be here.

JUNIE: Sorry. I didn't get the memo.

PUMA: Fuck.

JUNIE: I could go now.

PUMA: No, Crackmama should be here soon. She'll know what to do. There's some teacher Crackmama is always talking about frying her balls.

JUNIE: That's somebody else.

PUMA: I don't know.

JUNIE: Oh. Definitely. For sure. I don't have balls. And I don't even know Crackmama.

PUMA: She doesn't come to school much.

JUNIE: Why am I not surprised?

PUMA: You still coulda pissed her off. You're pissing me off. And Crackmama, she gets pissed off easy.

JUNIE: Technically, if she wants to discuss something with me, she's supposed to make an appointment – *(off PUMA's glare)* but I'm not a real stickler for the technical details.

PUMA: *(of the wall clock)* That the right time?

JUNIE: A couple of minutes slow.

PUMA: She shoulda been here then. Damn, I was supposed do a break in, do a tag, and then Crackmama was going to tell me the last thing. For my jumping in.

JUNIE: Jumping in?

PUMA: Yeah, to be part of the set.

JUNIE: Ah, an initiation ritual.

PUMA: The last one is usually something big.

JUNIE: Big?

PUMA: Yeah, big. Big. Torching a store or killing somebody or something.

JUNIE: I'm starting to like the sound of 'or something.'

PUMA: Damn. Bitch. One – I don't like it that you got a look at my face.

JUNIE: I wouldn't let that worry you. You're not that memorable. *(ignores PUMA'S scowl)* What's your name?

PUMA: Puma. *(as soon as the words are out of her mouth)* Fuck!

JUNIE: Don't worry. You're probably not listed in the school records under "Puma" since it's not your real name anyway. My name is Junie. I'd shake hands or fist bump, but...

PUMA: So, lady, what do you teach?

JUNIE: I teach Math.

PUMA; Math, oh man. That's like the worst.

JUNIE: Thanks.

PUMA: I mean, it's like the one class I couldn't get at all.

JUNIE: Because you're afraid of the material.

PUMA: Hey! I'm not afraid of nothin'?

JUNIE: You're probably very tough about torching and hair pulling and scratching other girls with your nails, but you are afraid of Mathematics. Don't feel bad about it. Most of the people in this country, adults *and* kids, have Math fear.

PUMA: I'm telling you, bitch, I'm not afraid.

JUNIE: Good. You see that tennis ball on my desk?

PUMA: Yeah.

JUNIE: Pick it up. Bounce it a few times.

PUMA: *(cautiously)* What is this?

JUNIE: You're not afraid to bounce a ball?

(PUMA *tentatively picks up the ball, bounces it on the floor, then again.*)

PUMA: Yeah.

JUNIE: Bounce it against the blackboard.

(PUMA *tosses the ball at the blackboard, catches it on the rebound.*)

PUMA: So.

JUNIE: Okay, here's your problem. Throw the ball away from you so it stops and comes right back to you. But it can't hit a wall or the floor or any object.

PUMA: What?

JUNIE: Throw the ball – if we were outside I'd say throw it as far and as hard as you can – make it stop and come straight back to you, without touching a wall, the floor or any object.

PUMA: That's impossible.

JUNIE: You sure? I know you can solve problems, Puma. The building is locked now, but you broke in, right? And you didn't set off the silent alarm.

PUMA: *(suddenly panicked)* Silent alarm?

JUNIE: No, I'm messing with you. There's no silent alarm, but there is an alarm and it didn't go off, so you figured out how to get around that.

PUMA: Yeah, well somebody told me.

JUNIE: Right. Okay. Nevertheless, think about this problem for more than half a second.

PUMA: This a Math problem?

JUNIE: It's a problem in logical thinking.

(PUMA *thinks, shrugs.*)

JUNIE: *(cont'd)* If you untie me, I'll show you.

PUMA: Like I'm going to fall for that.

JUNIE: Ah, signs of logical thinking. Okay, so first, state the problem.

PUMA: Throw the ball.

JUNIE: Hard.

PUMA: Hard.

JUNIE: But you're indoors, so not too hard. And don't throw like a girl.

(PUMA *mimes throwing the ball.*)

PUMA: This is crazy.

JUNIE: Not if you *think.* Just imagine you're outside on the baseball diamond and throw the ball as hard as you can toward the outfield. What happens?

PUMA: It just goes and goes.

JUNIE: Forever?

PUMA: 'Course not. It goes 'til it falls. Unless, like you could put a string or, hey, some like rubbery bungie or something on it. You could throw it and it'd come back. There, problem solved. Big deal.

JUNIE: Nothing can be attached to the ball.

PUMA: You didn't say that.

JUNIE: I should have said that.

PUMA: Then it's fucking crazy, lady.

JUNIE: Think.

PUMA: I have.

JUNIE: Not enough. A good thing to do when you're trying to solve a problem is play around with the elements, get familiar with it.

(PUMA *throws the ball against the blackboard, catches it on the rebound. She bounces it.*)

JUNIE: *(cont'd)* Yeah, like that.

(PUMA tosses the ball in the trash.)

JUNIE: Swish. Nothing but net.

(PUMA fishes the ball out, tosses it up and down in her hand. Suddenly a big grin spreads across her face.)

PUMA: Throw the ball? It's gotta stop in the air and come straight back to me, right?

JUNIE: That's right.

(PUMA tosses the ball straight up as high as conditions in the venue allow. It drops straight back into her palm.)

PUMA: *(a little defensively)* Whatever you say, woman, that did everything you asked.

JUNIE: It did.

PUMA: It did.

JUNIE: It did. I'm agreeing. You solved it. That's the answer.

(Inadvertently, PUMA grins broadly, very pleased. Then she catches herself, gets a more stern expression back on.)

JUNIE: *(cont'd)* Okay, now look at the blackboard, the part you didn't mess up with your vandalism.

PUMA: What for?

JUNIE: Afraid again? *(scary voice)* O-o-o-oh, there might be a math problem.

PUMA: Shut up.

(But JUNIE waits and eventually PUMA sneaks a quick glance at the board.)

PUMA: *(cont'd)* There's a bunch of dots.*

JUNIE: It's the warm up for tomorrow's first class. Your problem is to draw four straight lines, parallel to each other and the same distance from each other, so that there are two black dots in each section.

PUMA: It's not my problem.

JUNIE: Humor me.

PUMA: I don't have to.

JUNIE: It's the last request of woman before she dies. It's the least you can do.

(PUMA *draws some lines dividing the square, but nothing seems to work.*)

JUNIE: *(cont'd)* I wasn't sure you'd know what parallel means. You must have been paying attention at some point. That's excellent, Puma.

(PUMA *draws a couple more lines, then throws the chalk down.*)

PUMA: It's impossible.

JUNIE: There's that word again.

PUMA: Well, look at it!

JUNIE: It's impossible with the assumptions you're making. I said the lines have to be parallel to each other but not to the side of the rectangle. And the areas of the sections don't have to be the same.

PUMA: Fuck!

(*She goes and sits on a chair to the side. She and* JUNIE *both study the board. After a while,* PUMA *gets up and goes back to the problem. She erases her earlier lines, gets a piece of chalk – or marker – and draws the four lines that solve the puzzle. She looks at* JUNIE *expectantly.*)

JUNIE: *(smiling)* That's it.

(*Again* PUMA can't help a big, spontaneous smile.)

JUNIE: *(cont'd)* Puma, you've got some stuff. You can do math, and you can do school. And I can give you the statistics on your improved chances of getting a guy, having a family, and making good money, but. . .I know, quit while I'm ahead,. No statistics. So let's stick with the bottom line: do it, girl.

(*The funky music of* PUMA'S *cell phone sounds. She answers quickly.*)

PUMA: Yeah?. . .Right. . .Totally. . .Okay. *(clicks off)* Crackmama is here.

(JUNIE looks away, genuinely worried. PUMA studies her, wrestling with confusing thoughts, then comes to a decision. She produces a switchblade, pops it open. She moves quickly to JUNIE an d slices the phone wire. JUNIE rubs he hands to get the circulation back.)

PUMA: *(cont'd)* Get up, woman. Hurry. Go.

JUNIE: *(standing)* If I go, aren't you going to have a problem with Crackmama?

PUMA: Whatever. Get the hell out of here. Now!

JUNIE: What'll you do?

PUMA: Go! I'll figure something out.

JUNIE: Yes. *(hurries to the door, stops; then, with real admiration and respect)* Yes, I'm sure you will.

(PUMA gives JUNIE a look, both appreciative and warning, and JUNIE goes.)

BLACKOUT

THE END

Appendix

The Dot Problem

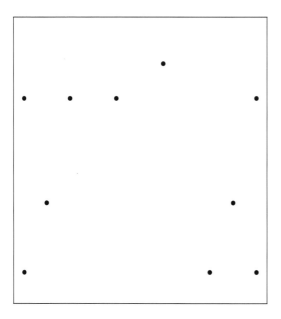

The problem: On the diagram of ten dots in the box, draw four straight lines, parallel to each other and equal distance from each other cutting the rectangle into five sections, with two dots in each section.

Hint 1: The lines must be parallel to each. There is no requirement that they be parallel to the top, bottom, or sides of the rectangle.

Hint 2: The four lines must be equal distance apart. There is no requirement that they enclose equal areas, i.e. there is no requirement that the five sections each be the same size.

Gold Star Mother

by Cynthia Robinson

Produced by manhattan**theatre**source *in Group A of EstroGenius 2012 with the following cast and crew:*

Director: Allison Moody

Ann Davenport: Cindy Keiter*

Pastor Robert Davenport: Alan Hasnas

Sound Designer: Amber Gallery

Lighting Designer: Kayla Goble

Stage Manager: Katt Masterson

Costume Designer: Julija Frodina

*Member of Actors' Equity Association

CONTACT
CynthiaGRobinson@gmail.com

CHARACTERS

FEMALE: Late 40's-early 50's; Pastor's wife; refined; outspoken

MALE: Late 40's-Early 50's; a Pastor; physically-imposing; a gifted orator

Note: The term "Gold Star Mother" refers to any mother who has lost a child in the service of the United States Armed Forces.

Mother's Day 2011. Sunday morning. A bedroom. ANN DAVENPORT *is dressed in all black. As she sits on a bed she folds a pile of laundry from a laundry basket. Periodically , she clutches garments to her chest, inhaling the scent of the clothing, as she sings a lullaby.*

ANN: *(singing)*
SLEEP WELL MY BABY
SLEEP WELL, MY SON
REST YOUR SWEET BODY
THE DAY IS DONE
MAY YOU BE PEACEFUL
YOUR SPIRIT LIGHT
SLEEP WELL , MY BABY
BE WELL. GOOD NIGHT.

Enter ANN'S *husband,* PASTOR ROBERT DAVENPORT, *dressed in a dark suit and clergy shirt. He is holding a lily plant. The serenity of* ANN'S *private moment is interrupted by* ROBERT'S *presence.*

ROBERT: The congregation missed you at church today.

ANN: The congregation missed me?

ROBERT: I missed you. You said you were coming to the 11 o'clock service.

ANN: I know. I was just about to leave but then I looked around and looked at this house and I just couldn't leave it like this.

ROBERT: Like what?

ANN: Like what? Can't you see it's a mess?

ROBERT: No.

ANN: Well, it is. And you know how much I hate to leave when everything is so out of place.

ROBERT: Ann, the house is fine.

ANN: *(ignoring her husband)* Once I stated cleaning this place up I couldn't stop and before I knew it was noon and I didn't think it would look right for the Pastor's wife to walk in late. You know how church folks like to talk.

ROBERT: I don't care about that. I was really hoping you'd come this week. I kept looking down from the pulpit, staring at your empty spot. I so wanted you to be there.

ANN: I'm sorry. I just couldn't make it. Maybe next week.

ROBERT: God willing.

ANN: Yeah.

A beat.

ANN: *(cont'd)* So how was the service?

ROBERT: Good. The Women's Club gave lilies for Mother's day. I saved this one for you. *He hands her the plant.*

ANN: It's beautiful. Thank you.

A beat. ANN reluctantly leans in and gives her husband an awkward kiss on the cheek. She places the plant on the dresser.

ANN: *(cont'd)* How was your sermon?

ROBERT: The congregation seemed pleased.

ANN: What did you decide on for this week?

ROBERT: "The Virgin Mary: A Mother's Love and the Virtue of her Faith."

ANN: Ahh, yes, that Mary certainly was the mother of all mothers.

ROBERT: Speaking of which, can't you do all of this tomorrow? It's supposed to be your day.

ANN: Mother's Day or not, chores have to be done. Laundry never ceases. You know Samuel hates it when he doesn't have a clean shirt to wear.

ROBERT: Ann, but today?

ANN: He would never think to do it for himself, but he loves clean laundry, that' for sure.

ROBERT: Ann—

ANN: --I know I've spoiled that boy but maybe one day he'll learn to do for himself, hopefully before he gets married.

ROBERT: Have you eaten lunch yet?

ANN: Robert, I told you I've been busy all morning. There's been so much to do here I haven't had a chance to think about food.

ROBERT: I made us a reservation at that place you like on Lawton Street. Thought we could have a little lunch date and then spend the rest of the afternoon together.

ANN: I don't know, I've got another load of laundry in the dryer, it won't be done for at least another twenty minutes and —

ROBERT: --Ok, so we can go in twenty minutes then.

ANN: I'm going to have to do something about that kitchen floor. There are few things I hate more than a dirty, sticky floor.

ROBERT: Ann —

ANN: --Samuel must have spilled some juice or something. He was probably in a rush , as usual, and didn't clean up after himself. I'm going to have to talk to him about these bad habits.

ROBERT gently takes a garment from his wife's hands and places it in the basket. He pulls her close, embracing her. She is visibly uncomfortable.

ROBERT: All of this can wait. Why don't you put on that pink and white dress I bought you? You look lovely in that. We'll go and have nice, long, relaxing meal, and then maybe we can come back here and---

ANN abruptly releases herself from ROBERT'S embrace.

ANN: ---No. I mean, I'm not really hungry right now.

ROBERT: It's a beautiful day. We can walk to the restaurant and work up an appetite.

ANN: I really ought to get this done.

ROBERT: Ok, then I'll help you.

He sits on the bed and begins to fold laundry, much to ANN'S dismay.

ROBERT: *(cont'd)* Four hand are better than two, right? It'll get done a lot faster this way and then we can work in a little fun, maybe even take in a movie. Remember all those movies we used to see?

He leans over to kiss his wife's neck. ANN *rises.*

ANN: That was a long time ago.

A beat.

ANN: *(cont'd)* You know, I finally figured out why Samuel's asthma had been worsening at night. It's all the dust that accumulates in this room. I don't even know how he's been able to stand it this long. I mean look at this.

She swipes the night stand, conducting a "white glove test" and shows it to ROBERT.

ANN: *(cont'd)* Disgusting, right? ˋ

ROBERT: I don't see a thing.

ANN: You never do. I don't know how I let this get away from me. As his mother the least I could do is make sure his room is free of dust.

She returns to folding clothes and discovers some socks with holes in them.

ROBERT: Can you please just----

ANN: ---Now will you look at these. I don't know how anyone can wear socks like this. Looks like I have some sewing to do today as well. Goodness, this is going to be a long afternoon.

ROBERT: Ann, please stop----

ANN: ----Don't let me stop you. You should get something to eat. You've had a long morning and I'm sure you must be hungry.

ROBERT: I want you to come with me. I need you with me.

ANN: Don't be silly. I'll be here when you get back. You can bring me something. You choose, you know what I like.

A beat.

ROBERT: He's not coming back.

ANN: What?

ROBERT: You don't have to do all of this because...he's not coming back.

ANN stops folding and glares at ROBERT.

ANN: Don't you ever say that to me again

She returns to folding her clothes.

ROBERT: It's the truth.

ANN: Robert, just go.

ROBERT: Have you called Dr. Thomas?

ANN: No need for that.

ROBERT: I think you should make another appointment.

ANN: I've given that man enough of our hard-earned money as it is, don't you think?

ROBERT: I don't care about the money, I care about you.

ANN: I am fine.

ROBERT: Some members of the church have formed a support group. They meet on Wednesday nights. Perhaps you'd like to join them?

ANN becomes increasingly agitated.

ANN: I do not want to join them. I don't want to talk to a bunch of strangers.

ROBERT: They're not strangers, they're our congregation.

ANN: They know nothing about me.

A beat.

ANN: *(cont'd)* Now, if you don't mind I'd really like to finish this. I cannot live in clutter and chaos, I want this room to be clean, I want my floors to be clean, I want this house to be clean, and I want my son to have fresh shirts and socks to wear, is that so terrible? That's what a good mother does.

ANN resumes folding, ROBERT grabs her wrists, stopping her from folding more clothes.

ROBERT: Stop this!

ANN: Robert, please---

ROBERT: ---I've had enough of this foolishness. Now you're going to change your clothes and come with me.

ANN releases herself.

ANN: I will do no such thing. If only your congregation could see you now.

ROBERT grabs her again.

ROBERT: I've had enough! You are my wife and you are coming with me now.

ANN: No, stop —

A frustrated ROBERT grabs the laundry basket from his wife and throws it onto the floor. ANN calmly kneels and puts the clothes back into the basket as ROBERT stands over her.

ROBERT: Samuel is DEAD.

ANN: You don't know that.

ROBERT: I do know and so do you.

ANN: No I don't.

ROBERT kneels before his wife.

ROBERT: *(cautiously)* They came and told us. Remember?

ANN: I don't know what you are talking about.

ROBERT: Six months ago---

ANN: ---I don't want to hear this---

ROBERT: ---two army officers came to our door. They told us about our Samuel and what happened to him.

ANN: Shut your mouth!

ROBERT: We went to Good Hope Cemetery.

ANN: Don't!

ROBERT: And we had a funeral.

ANN: Why are you doing this?! Why are you being so cruel?

ROBERT; And we buried our son.

ANN: *(shaken)* No we didn't! We did not bury him! We did no such thing!

ROBERT: Yes Ann, we had a funeral and----

ANN: ---We went to Good Hope Cemetery and we had a funeral, but we did not bury my son! We did not bury my Samuel! We buried a cold, hard, empty wooden box, that's what we buried! That's what we put in that ground! Not my son! Not my Samuel! That box was empty! So you see, you're confused! You've got it all wrong!

ROBERT: Ann, that box was empty because there was nothing left of him to bury.

In an effort to busy herself she begins a frantic pacing, dusting and straightening up of the room.

ROBERT: *(cont'd)* How long do you plan to wait for him?

ANN: He's my son.

ROBERT: You need to listen to me, you must accept the fact that Samuel----

ANN: ----HE'S MY SON! I'M HIS MOTHER AND HE'S MY SON AND HE'S A PART OF ME AND I'M A PART OF HIM! I CARRIED HIM INSIDE OF ME AND I FEEL LIKE HE'S STILL THERE! IF HE IS DEAD, SO AM I!

She cries. ROBERT embraces her.

ROBERT: No, Ann. That's where you're wrong. You're very much alive, we both are, and I need you to be with me, I need you now.

ANN: I cannot be what you need me to be right now.

ROBERT: You're my wife and I'm your husband and we need each other now more than ever. We have to move on, together.

ANN: Move on? Without Samuel? I can't.

ROBERT: Ann—

ANN: ---You just preached to a church full of people about Mary and faith...Where's your faith, PASTOR? Why don't you believe? People look to you for hope and spiritual guidance and you don't even have faith yourself, faith in your own son's life. Shame on you.

ROBERT: I have faith that my son is in a better place.

ANN: There's no better place for him than here with me.

ROBERT: He's with God. He's with his Heavenly Father and that's the best place he can be. God will help us through this. Our faith in the Lord is all we have right now. Without it we are dead. Come, Ann, pray with me.

ROBERT drops to his knees and invites ANN to pray with him. He tries to pull her down, but she resists.

ANN: *(bitterly)* Don't you dare ask me to do that. I'm done praying. I've clung to my faith for 19 years. Ever since I gave birth to Samuel, ever since the doctor placed that tiny little boy in my arms I've been praying for him. I've prayed for my son every day of his life and I believed with all my heart that God would keep safe. All I had to do was be a good mother, a good wife, a good Christian and He'd keep my boy safe. But it was all a lie. God did not keep His promise to me! I will never get on my knees again for as long as I live. Don't you ever ask me to do that again!

ROBERT: We cannot question God's will. We can only believe that what happens is for the best, and there is a blessing here, we just have to be still and listen for it.

ANN: You can believe that bullshit if you want to---

ROBERT: ---Ann, don't you use that language in my house---

ANN: ---This is my house, too! Face it, the Heavenly father is a fairy tale. A lie I've believed in all my life...until now. Now I know the truth.

ROBERT: That is blasphemous talk. You don't mean what you're saying.

ANN: Don't you tell me about what I mean PASTOR. You may be the head of a congregation but you obviously know nothing about being a husband and father.

ROBERT: Damn you, Ann! You have no right! He was my son too!

ANN: Listen to yourself. You call yourself a man of God? The truth is your God...this so-called Father in heaven...Holy Spirit...Holy Ghost, whatever you want to call Him, He stole by baby from me.

ROBERT: YOU CAN'T BLAME GOD. WHAT IS WRONG WITH YOU? WE'RE AT WAR. Read your bible, Ann. You'd be able to understand all of this if you were really a faithful servant, if you were a true student of scripture. This is not the first time the righteous have been called on to carry out God's will against the wicked.

ANN: My son was killed and there's nothing righteous about that. I don't give a shit about God's will. There's nothing righteous about the death of a young boy.

ANN collapses into sobs.

ANN: *(cont'd) (hysterically)* Are you happy now, Pastor? I said it. Samuel is dead and he's never coming back. I will never see my son again! My beautiful son was blown to bits in some desert thousands of miles away from his home and the child I gave birth to is just dust somewhere and I will never be able to hold him, or touch him, or smell him, or talk to him ever again. Are you satisfied? I've accepted it! Hallelujah! Hallelujah!

ROBERT kneels to pray. He struggles to hold back tears.

ROBERT: Dear God, I ask that you bless my wife with peace of mind. I ask that you bless her spirit with the strength to maintain her faith in the face of the loss of her...of our...son. I ask that You give me the strength to...Samuel, can you hear me? It's daddy. I love you, son...I miss you...I want you to know that...I wish you were here and...Oh, God, please help me...help, Lord...help me...please.

ROBERT is overcome with emotion. He can no longer pray and instead collapses into violent sobs. ANN kneels with ROBERT and embraces him.

THE END

Redemption

by Lisa Bruna

Produced by manhattan**theatre**source *in Group B of EstroGenius 2012 with the following cast and crew:*

Director: Jessica McVea

He: Matthew Trumbull

She: Kate Dickinson

Sound Designer: Madeleine Gaw

Lighting Designer: R. S. Buck

Stage Manager: Pat Lewis

CONTACT

lisabruna17@gmail.com
www.lisabruna.com

CHARACTERS

HE: a mindful man (late20s-early 30s

SHE: a wily woman (late 20s-early 30s)

Summer evening. Inside the Triple-Decker Deli. HE *sits alone at a table set for two with sandwiches on plates at each side.* SHE *enters, looks around.* HE *slinks slowly down in his seat as* SHE *approaches his table.*

HE: Oh no, no, no, no, no, no. You have got to be kidding me.

SHE: *(cheerfully)* Hey there.

HE: What are you doing here?

SHE: I came to see you.

HE: How'd you know where...

SHE: Ah, turkey club on rye. It must be Thursday. *(peeking at the other plate)* Looks like SHE's having avocado and Swiss on whole wheat. Good god, are those sprouts?

HE: Sorry I can't ask you to join us. I wouldn't want you to feel as if you're shamelessly intruding upon my life.

SHE: *(sits in the chair opposite him)* Mind if I sit?

HE: Very much so.

SHE: *(taking a closer look at the food in front of her)* She orders the fruit salad instead of chips? What are we dealing with here, a health nut? An environmentalist? Let me guess – she drives a Prius.

HE: You have no idea what you're talking about.

SHE: I'm talking about your date.

HE: Who said this was a date?

SHE: You're wearing your striped polo.

HE: So?

SHE: It's your date shirt.

HE: It's also my end-of-the clean-laundry-pile, takin'-care-of-business casualwear. For all you know, I'm causally conducting a covert operation for an organized crime enterprise I run in my spare time.

SHE: Nah...you're not nearly that fascinating. AND you're not that hard to figure out. Today is your second payday of the month, you're rocking the striped polo, and you reek of Drakkar. I'm willing to bet you've got a fresh pack of minty green Tic Tacs in your pants pocket. This is a bona fide date all right.

HE: You're unbelievable. You think you're so clever.

SHE: So where is she? *(looking around)* You didn't scare her away already, did you? *(She plucks a grape from the plate and pops it in her mouth)* Does she know you're a dork? Oh god, you didn't bring up your fossil collection, did you?

HE: She knows nothing of my fossils. And I did not scare her away. She's in the restroom.

SHE: Aha, so this IS a date.

HE: *(reluctantly)* Fine. It's a date. But you're way off on everything else. She knows nothing of my fossils. And I don't have Tic Tacs in my pocket.

SHE: So tell me more about her. We already know she's a sprout-lover. What else? Does save baby seals? Does she listen to indie rock? Ooh, I bet she thinks you're like totally awesome.

HE: I know what you're getting at. Yes, she's young. But she's very mature. She's a bright young woman with an excellent career.

SHE: An income earner. That's different. What does she do?

HE: She's a model. A catalog model.

SHE: Ooh la la... Victoria's Secret?

HE: J.C. Penney *(beat)* I'm sorry. Why are you still here?

SHE: A model, huh? *(eating another grape)* And you're wooing her with grilled sandwiches at the Triple Decker Deli? No wonder the poor girl is in the toilet.

HE: You're jealous.

SHE: I'm just trying to help you.

HE: Help me?

SHE: Trust me, you could use a few tips if you want this to pan out. You're not exactly off to a great start. I mean, you brought this girl to a sandwich place. *(noticing that he is not catching on)* Where CARBS live?

HE: YOU always liked it here.

SHE: Don't you know anything? *(holding up his date's sandwich)* THIS...is model kryptonite. She's probably purging in the powder room as we speak.

HE: *(glances at his watch looks in the direction of the rest rooms)* She has been in there a long time. *(growing visibly perturbed)* Again, why are you here?

SHE: Oh, I'm glad you reminded me. You'll never guess what I found in your sock drawer.

HE: I don't have a sock drawer. I have a sock milk crate.

SHE: When we lived together, you had a sock drawer.

HE: And a constant headache.

SHE: I'm being serious.

HE: So am I.

SHE: Okay, let's start over. I want to make this fun. Close your eyes.

HE: I don't trust you.

SHE: Yes, you do. Close your eyes.

(HE reluctantly complies. SHE places a home-made printed greeting card decorated with a big red heart on the table in front of him.)

Okay, now open 'em.

HE: What's this?

SHE: Read it.

HE: *(reading)* Happy Valentine's Day. *(looking up at her)* It's August.

SHE: Read the bottom part.

HE: *(reading)* This coupon entitles the bear...the BEAR?

SHE: Obviously, it's supposed to say bear-ER. It's a typo. Move on.

HE: Okay...This coupon entitles the bear...*(laughs)*

SHE: Stop it! Keep reading.

HE: Okay, okay...this coupon entitles the bear-ER to one full night of sizzling hot ... *(reads to himself, murmuring)* ...with a sensual... and an extra dose of...WHOA!

SHE: I know...WHOA...right? So I found it tucked all the way in the back of your drawer. Can you believe this was...us?

HE: *(suddenly turned on)* I'm not sure. Sometimes I have a hard time remembering which was the REAL 'us' and which was the stuff-I-visualized-daily-but-never-got-the-courage-to-actually-DO 'us'.

SHE: I can only imagine how such ... activities ... must have played out in that head of yours.

HE: *(looking at the card again, grinning)* Wow! *(He locks eyes with her.)* I'm a little fuzzy on the details. Did we actually DO this? *(He points to a line on the coupon.)* For real?

SHE: We actually did ... not.

HE: *(his bubble bursts)* What? Why?

SHE: *(taking the card back from him)* The coupon was never redeemed.

HE: How do you know?

SHE: *(waving the card, fanning herself)* First of all, I'm pretty sure I would remember if we'd done something like...this.

HE: *(obviously turned on)* True. But I seem to remember that we did an awful lot of...things...that would most likely have led up to...that.

SHE: Wellll, we certainly did so some...things. *(She gazes at him coyly)*

HE: Hmmm.

SHE: Hmmm what?

HE: *(gazing back at her)* I'd forgotten how sexy you can be.

SHE: Hmmm. *(SHE smiles at him for a moment, lost in his deliberate gaze.)*

HE: So what's the second thing?

SHE: What second thing?

HE: You said 'first of all,' which means you must have a 'second of all' in there somewhere...if I remember what makes you tick... *(smiling suggestively)*...and I think I do.

SHE: Oh! Right! Okay, look at the back. *(SHE turns the card over and shows it to him as she reads.)* See? It says, Upon redemption, the bearer – and, congratulations, you spelled it right this time – the bearer will receive...

HE: *(HE takes over.)* The bearer will receive three consecutive deeply intense...*(He continues reading to himself, murmuring the words inaudibly.)* ... WHOA!"

SHE: Right? *(SHE returns his gaze, then breaks their mutual trance.)* And we both know THAT never happened.

(They both think about the lost opportunity, then simultaneously sigh.)

HE: Wait a minute, what did you mean when you said I spelled it right this time? Are you suggesting I gave this coupon to YOU?

SHE: Yup, I'm the bear! *(SHE curls her raised hands like bear claws.)* Raaaawr!

HE: Hmm, that can't be right.

SHE: Okay, let me clarify. YOU wrote the Valentine and gave it to ME. For whatever reason, I never redeemed it. Oh well. Case closed.

HE: Ah, yes. There's that tone I remember. You're right. I'm wrong. No discussion.

SHE: What's to discuss? You just admitted that you lived half of our time together in some fantasy world inside your brain. I, on the other hand, was fully present and living in reality at all times.

HE: Except for the 10 months when you were taking those *(he makes air quotes with his fingers)* 'vitamins' that made you act a bit...out of character.

SHE: Those were herbs. All natural. They were prescribed...

HE: By your witch-doctor friend...doesn't count. And she even said there might be side effects.

SHE: Side effects like writing suggestive Valentine coupons and then having no memory of writing them?

HE: You did do some crazy things as I recall.

SHE: So now you're calling me crazy?

HE: Welllll, if you want to know the truth...

SHE: Truth, huh? What would YOU know about truth?

HE: *(standing)* Look, I'm the most honest person you'll ever meet.

SHE: *(SHE stands and leans toward him across the table.)* Oh, yeah?

HE: *(HE leans in closer to her. They are nose to nose.)* Yeah.

SHE: *(SHE presses up against him.)* Honest?

HE: *(HE slides his hand up her back.)* To a fault.

(SHE slips her hand into his front pants pocket and slowly pulls out a box of green Tic Tacs. While holding his gaze, still nose to nose with him, SHE gently rattles the box of candies and speaks in a slow, steady tone.)

SHE: Then what are these doing in your pocket?

HE: *(HE leans in closer. They are still nose to nose, breathing heavily.)* Okay, so I'm busted. Ya got me. I'm a big...fat...liar.

SHE: *(slowly, intensely)* Your pants are so on fire.

HE: *(slowly, intensely)* You have no idea.

SHE: *(slowly, intensely)* You still want to talk to me about honesty?

HE: *(slowly, intensely)* Mmm hmm...I'm prepared to be so honest with you right now.

SHE: *(coyly)* Ooooh, and I'm ready to be honest with you too.

HE: *(slowly, intensely)* Oh, yeah?

SHE: *(sensuously)* Oh YEAH, baby. I want you to know...and I mean this from the bottom of my heart...*(She slowly slides her hand down his arm, presses the Tic Tac box into his hand, then raises his hand to face level.)* Baby...you.....could really use one of these. *(She steps away, laughing, leaving him in a state of interrupted seduction.)*

HE: That is SO unfair.

(As he shakes it off, he notices she is headed toward the rest room.)

Hey! Where are you going?"

SHE: *(playfully)* Just need to powder my nose.

HE: *(jumping to block her way to the rest room door)* Whoa, whoa, whoa. Your nose does not need to go poking around in there.

(He places his hands gently on her shoulders and guides her back to the table. He sits her down in the chair then returns to his own chair.)

Now, let's get to the bottom of this mysterious love coupon. Isn't that why you're here?

SHE: Oh, NOW you're interested.

HE: I've always been interested. I mean... I don't know if you realize it, but this ... this ... delicate little artifact that you carefully excavated from the back of a sock drawer is like ... well, it's like a romantic relic left behind as physical evidence of our ... our ....

SHE: Yes...?

HE: Of our ....

SHE: You still can't say it, can you?

HE: I CAN say it. I choose not to. I don't see the need to dig up ancient history.

SHE: You spend your life digging up ancient history. It's what you do.

HE: *(taking a closer look at the card)* Well, then ... as long as we're digging things up, here's a clue – there's no way in hell I would have used Comic Sans. You know how much I hate that font.

SHE: Yeah, well I hate it too. EVERYBODY hates that font. You've proved nothing.

HE: Hmm...fair enough.

SHE: Here's a clue for YOU! There's no way I would ever make the mistake of writing BEAR. You know that. *(She takes a small bite of the sandwich in front of her.)*

HE: Perhaps you forget to use spell check that day.

SHE: Spell check wouldn't have caught BEAR .... it's an actual word.

HE: Well there you go then! A spell-check oversight. That explains the mistake.

SHE: I don't make spelling mistakes.

HE: Ah yes, I forgot. You're perfect. *(half to himself)* She never makes mistakes.

SHE: Oh! I've made mistakes all right. But at least I've always been honest.

HE: Here we go again. Look, if you have something to say...

SHE: *(SHE stands and heads back toward the restroom.)* I need a tissue.

HE: *(chasing after her)* No you don't! Here, use a napkin. *(He gets to the rest room first and plants himself in front of the door.)*

SHE: What are you afraid I'll find in there? *(beat)*...or not find.

HE: *(suspicious)* What are you implying exactly?

SHE: Come on now. You know I've always been able to see right through you.

HE: Maybe just this once, you can stop looking THROUGH me and just look AT me. *(beat)* I'm just trying to go about my business and get on with my life the best I can.

SHE: If by 'your business' you mean the drugstore redhead I passed in the parking lot making snarky remarks on her cell phone ... something about walking out on her blind date with a lame paleontologist ... then okay. But I'm guessing she's also getting on with HER life, and it doesn't include calling YOU ever again.

HE: *(heading back to the table)* What happened to us?

SHE: *(following him)* I told you – models don't eat sandwiches. *(beat)* But don't worry about it. You can do so much better than her. She didn't deserve you, you know.

HE: No, I mean ... what happened to US us?

SHE: I don't know. We used to see eye to eye on everything. *(She eats another grape.)*

HE: We were so in tune. We used to...

SHE: "finish" each other's sentences.

HE: Now you're finishing my date's dinner.

SHE: She wasn't going to eat this. Too much fructose.

HE: *(laughing weakly)* No, and she probably wasn't going to appreciate my fossils either.

SHE: She definitely wouldn't have organized your sock drawer.

HE: *(waving the card)* And, let's face it, she wasn't the type of girl who was going to chase me down eighteen months later to quibble over a mysterious love coupon.

SHE: *(playfully)* Nah, she didn't look sharp enough to even understand the value of a clever little document like this.

HE: Which, I have to admit, IS quite clever. *(HE stands, slides her chair away from the table, extends his arm and begins leading her out of the deli.)*Whoever wrote this is pretty damn sharp ....BUT they seem to have left off one particular detail regarding the redemption of this thing.

SHE: Oh yeah? What's that?

HE: *(smiles and hands her the card as if for the first time)* There's no expiration date.

(HE reaches in his pocket for the Tic Tacs and pops one in his mouth. SHE smiles seductively and wraps her arm snugly around his. They exit arm in arm.)

BLACKOUT

THE END

Orangutan & Lulu

by Lisa Kenner Grissom

Produced by manhattan**theatre**source *in Group B of EstroGenius 2012 with the following cast and crew:*

Director: Amanda Junco

Orangutan: Rusty Buehler

Lulu: Laura Butler*

Sound Designer: Madeleine Gaw

Lighting Designer: R. S. Buck

Stage Manager: Pat Lewis

*Member of Actors' Equity Association

CONTACT
lisa.kenner@gmail.com

CHARACTERS

ORANGUTAN-- man, 20's-40's. Likes his backyard, and doesn't see much reason to go beyond it. A little too comfortable in his skin, he needs a push now and then.

LULU-- woman, 20's-40's. Highly imaginative and enjoys challenging the status quo. Her sassiness belies an inner vulnerability.

Time/Place: Open to interpretation

Author's Notes
A slash (/) is overlapping dialogue.
A dash (--) is interrupted dialogue.
Although the characters in this text are 20's – 40's, characters can be any age.
Characters can be any ethnicity.

The space is spare except for a few objects that make this place a home.

ORANGUTAN *(man, 20's)* holds LULU *(woman, 20's) tightly in his arms.*

They are intertwined. They might be lying on a bed, a couch, or something lounge-y. They might be standing against a wall. Wherever they are...

A pool of light surrounds and encloses them.

ORANGUTAN: Lulu?

LULU: Yes, Orangutan?

ORANGUTAN: You're too far away...

LULU: That's not/even possible.

ORANGUTAN: Can you come closer please? Just a little closer.

LULU: *(sincerely)* I don't think I can, Orangutan.

ORANGUTAN: Try.

LULU: Really, I don't—

ORANGUTAN: Just try!

LULU: Ok!

She moves a smidge closer. Or maybe she just moves around, as if to seem closer.

LULU: *(cont'd)* How's that?

ORANGUTAN: Modestly better.

LULU: But better?

ORANGUTAN: I don't know yet.

A moment.

ORANGUTAN: *(cont'd)* Yes, better.

LULU: Good.

ORANGUTAN: Good

They adjust. A bit more. And a bit more. Then, they settle.

ORANGUTAN: Lulu?

LULU: Yes?

ORANGUTAN: I love you.

LULU: I love you, too.

ORANGUTAN: I love you more.

LULU: No, you don't.

ORANGUTAN: I think I do.

LULU: That's not true.

ORANGUTAN: It might be.

LULU: I doubt it, O.

ORANGUTAN: But you can't say for sure.

LULU: One never knows for sure.

ORANGUTAN: About love?

LULU: About anything. *(beat)* What I know is this. You are here and I am here and we are together and we are very, very,VERY close.

ORANGUTAN: Emotionally.

LULU: Physically.

ORANGUTAN: That comforts me.

ORANGUTAN closes his eyes. LULU does not. She sighs audibly. A moment. Then, LULU starts to hyperventilate.

LULU: I CAN'T...BREATHE! I'm sweating. This is so confining! I need to...um...MOVE. Move away. JUST A BIT.

She frantically moves to get loose, until she gets loose. They both sigh in unison.

ORANGUTAN: Ok.

LULU: Ok?

ORANGUTAN: Yes, ok.

She sighs, a mix of surprise and relief.

LULU: Good! Great!

*The pool of lights expands as Lulu stretches her fingers and toes.
She luxuriates in these small movements.*

LULU: Ah. That feels SO good.

ORANGUTAN: Hmm?

LULU: To stretch. Doesn't it feel good? Even just a little bit.

ORANGUTAN: Not much of a stretch/er...

LULU: Try it!

ORANGUTAN: Ok. I'll give it/a go

The light expands, still enclosing them.

LULU: Oh do! C'est magnifique!

ORANGUTAN *moves ever so slightly. Then stops.*

LULU *uncurls his fingers which hold her. She stretches his hands out. Then
his toes. She positions his body like a snow angel.*

*She waits. Nothing.
Then she tries to move his arms and hands, to encourage him to make a
snow angel.*

ORANGUTAN: I'm not used to/someone

LULU: Just trust/me!

ORANGUTAN: I don't/WANT TO!!

LULU: JUST DO IT!!

*They each sigh or pant or grunt. They disentangle and separate.
The pool of light splits in two.*

Perhaps ORANGUTAN *sits up. Perhaps* LULU *stands against a wall.
A few moments pass.*

Then, LULU *moves as if she is making snow angels.*

LULU: I like making snow angels. Even when there is no snow.

ORANGUTAN: That makes no sense.

LULU: The feeling. Makes me feel little. Try it.

ORANGUTAN: I don't know how. Not a lot of snow where I'm from. Did you forget?

LULU: No. I just/

ORANGUTAN: How could you?

LULU: What?

ORANGUTAN: Forget.

LULU: I didn't. I just forgot to remember! I think it's sad. That you never made snow angels.

ORANGUTAN: No it's not.

LULU: I think it's sad. Can't I have my feelings?

ORANGUTAN: I think it's sad you've never seen the sun set over the cacti. Beautiful.

LULU: It's not the same thing.

ORANGUTAN: My love for cacti and your love for snow angles. No I suppose not. We're quite different in that regard.

The space/light between them widens a bit further.
They are in their own worlds.

ORANGUTAN: Lu?

LULU: Yes?

ORANGUTAN: Why did you start calling me Orangutan?

LULU: You know.

ORANGUTAN: Tell me again.

LULU: Because your hands were everywhere.

ORANGUTAN: Yes. *(beat)* You liked it...

LULU: I did. I do...but. There are times when...stillness is good, too. *(beat)* Why did you start calling me Lulu?

ORANGUTAN: Because you think you are French.

LULU: Oui. That's true. Deep in my soul. I am Francais.

ORANGUTAN: Even though you're not.

LULU: JE SUIS!!

ORANGUTAN: YOU ARE NOT!!

The space/light widens even further.
They are in their own worlds.
Moments pass. Time flies.
LULU *reaches out into the open space.*

LULU: Orangutan?

ORANGUTAN: Yes, Lulu?

LULU: Just checking.

ORANGUTAN: I'm here.

LULU: I miss you.

ORANGUTAN: I gave you room. To stretch.

LULU: I know. That was nice. I still miss you.

A moment.

ORANGUTAN: Don't make me do snow angels, ok? I don't know how to do it and I don't want to do it.

LULU: D'accord. *(beat)* That means, ok.

ORANGUTAN: I won't make you dream of suns setting over the cacti. I know cacti scare you.

LULU: They don't scare me.

ORANGUTAN: Ok. They don't scare you.

LULU: Well maybe a little.

ORANGUTAN: Come here.

They find each other.

ORANGUTAN: *(cont'd)* I won't wrap myself around you so you can't move. I'll just...

He invites her to nestle in beside him. She does.
They move until they eventually settle.
The light encloses them again, now in a wider circle.
They breathe. Together.

ORANGUTAN: Stay here. Oui?

LULU: Oui?!

ORANGUTAN: Oui.

They kiss.
The light expands to fill the entire space.
Then, blackout.

THE END

Destiny

by Patricia Henritze

Produced by manhattan**theatre**source *in Program B of EstroGenius 2012 with the following cast and crew:*

Director: Emma Duncan

Jody: Jenny Paul

May: Charlotte Foster

Sound Designer: Madeleine Gaw

Lighting Designer: R. S. Buck

Stage Manager: Pat Lewis

CONTACT
patriciahenritze@gmail.com

CHARACTERS
JODY—a young woman in her mid 20s
MAY--a young woman in her mid 20s

Time: Today

(Lights rise on two women sitting on a stoop drinking beer our of bottles. This particular stoop is in a small town in New Jersey, but it could be most anywhere in the US. JODY, 25, haphazardly wears a wedding dress and veil. MAY, 26, is in her best dress, her shoes are of. Off SR (or L, if that works better for you) we can hear music, the occasional crash. JODY stares out past the audience, as MAY fusses with the panty hose she's wearing. Empty beers and a couple of full ones are strewn about. An empty bottle of champagne lies on its side. In the course of the scene they finish their half drunk beers and open new ones.)

JODY: Remember snow? When you were a kid?

MAY: It still snows -

JODY: Winter? When you were little?

MAY: *(Yanking her hose)* I freakin' hate freakin' panty hose.

JODY: It was soft. Really soft.

MAY: What the hell is wrong with you? Do I remember snow?

JODY: I don't know…

(JODY tips her beer bottle straight up.)

MAY: I'm takin' em off.

(MAY struggles with her hose through the next few lines.)

JODY: It just seems like it doesn't snow good anymore. The kind you can make snowmen out of, and angels –

MAY: My sad little Eskimo.

JODY: Inuit.

MAY: What?

JODY: Inuits, May, Inuits.

MAY: Inuits?

JODY: They're not Eskimos, anymore. They're called Inuits. You should read a newspaper once in a while.

MAY: So there's no snow and no Eskimos?

(JODY looks off SR where we hear an extra bump of noise. A door slams and we hear "Whoo Hooo!! before the door slams again.)

JODY: God, look at him. He's drunk.

MAY: And you're not?

JODY: Not as drunk as he is -

MAY: Besides it's all like "Grandmother hammered to death in a 'home invasion' " or nuclear somethin' horrible or monkey virus.

(JODY looks at MAY confused.)

Newspapers - I hate reading them and I know what Inuits are.

JODY: It's bird virus now – they've been falling out of the sky for years –

MAY: And when did it become a 'home invasion'? Like the Marines broke into your house. *(beat)* Anyway, it's swine not bird.

JODY: No, that's flu. Swine flu. SO two years ago. If you read the paper you'd know -

MAY: And I'd still be out here with a drunken, depressed bride.

(Crash from SR.)

JODY: *(Looking SR)* Oh god. I'm not depressed. I'm suicidal.

MAY: Good. It will save you the pain of divorce.

JODY: Why do we wear panty hose anyway?

MAY: Only for your wedding, dear.

JODY: Thank you.

MAY: Anything for you.

JODY: You'll be married next.

MAY: Yeah, right.

JODY: Everybody gets married, May.

MAY: Whether they want to or not?

JODY: Pretty much.

MAY: Wow. To the happy bride.

(MAY toasts JODY with her beer bottle.)

JODY: If you could be anything you wanted, what would you be?

MAY: I can be anything I want.

JODY: No you can't.

MAY: When I was in fourth grade I wrote a paper saying I wanted to be the first lady president.

JODY: Mrs. Pandler's class?

MAY: Miss Tate.

JODY: Lady president.

MAY: Yeah. I only said it to impress her. She was so smart and she thought I was smart - I loved her.

JODY: You are smart. I mean, you're not the one sitting in the stupid white dress. You went out with him before I did.

MAY: He's a good guy.

(There's a loud crash and they look SR for a moment.)

A drunk guy, but a good guy. We were just friends.

JODY: You went out.

MAY: It was high school - he just wanted to talk about you.

JODY: So if you can be anything you want -

MAY: I can.

JODY: - and you sling drinks in a bar all day long -

MAY: Drunken slut, Sex on the beach, gimlets, ice teas and Martinis of every conceivable kind -

JODY: Then you must want to be a bartender. At Ray's? Out of all the jobs in the world?

MAY: Not a rocket scientist, not a river keeper, not a croissant baker -

JODY: You've chosen bartending.   It didn't just happen?

MAY: Exactly. It's my life. I live to pour. Wait, wait, wait – I've just invented a drink: The Suicidal Bride. It's champagne with a shot of Jaegermeister. It makes me want to kill myself just thinking of drinking it.

JODY: I think there's already a drink with Jaeger and –

MAY: Damn it. My one 'shot' at greatness.

JODY: So, wait, if I can be anything I want and I'm stuck out here in this dress -

MAY: Cascading veil and all.

JODY: Then I must want to be married to a drunken moron.

MAY: And be sitting here in a massive - but lovely - white dress.

JODY: So this is my dream come true?

MAY: Because everybody gets married -

JODY: Well they do.

MAY: Okay. Then, everything you ever did led up to this moment. This one right now.

(They pause somberly and drink.)

JODY: Then why aren't you married?

MAY: Because I never said that.   About everyone getting married. We're making destiny, baby. What you 'think' is 'who' you are. Yeah, you are what you think - or maybe what you drink or-

JODY: So every moment of your life led to what?

MAY: Besides the art of bartending?

(MAY really looks at JODY who's staring at the moon.)

Seeing you in a white dress with a drink in your hand and the moon just so. *(beat)* You're beautiful.

JODY: We could leave.

MAY: We could.

JODY: How long till someone noticed?

MAY: We've been out here almost an hour.

JODY: Nobody even came to look. I'm the bride.

MAY: I can see that.

JODY: I'm the bride and no one even came to check.

MAY: *(Quietly)* I came. To check.

JODY: Where could we go? If we run away, right now?

MAY: I'll take you anywhere.

(Off SR there's music blares in and the sound of screen door slams)

NEW HUSBAND: *(off stage)* JODY! JODY! Where are you? Come in and dance with me!

(Other voices are heard shouting to her, OS, as well: come in, let's dance, etc.)

JODY: *(jumping up and shouting SR)* I'll be in in a minute!

NEW HUSBAND: *(off stage)* JODY! JODY! Baby, come dance with me!!

JODY: *(still shouting SR)* Would somebody freakin' dance with him!!!!?

NEW HUSBAND: *(off stage)* I love you, Jody! I love you!!!

(Music trails off as door slams.) HUSBAND'S gone back inside.

JODY: He loves me. *(beat)* Will you take me to Alaska? Now. Before he comes back?

MAY: Honeymoon with the Inuits.

JODY: We can slide down glaciers.

MAY: I better put my panty hose back on - I'll need them for warmth.

JODY: And I'll be invisible in my white dress in the snow.

MAY: *(toasting the air)* To the legend of the drunken snow bride.

JODY: I'm already invisible.

MAY: Oh god. Are you always this whiny or is the veil too tight?

JODY: You brought me beer. I like beer.

MAY: I'm a bartender. I know intuitively when beer is needed.

JODY: Why did I marry him when I have you, May?

(She puts her head sleepily in May's lap.)

   Who needs a husband with friends like you...

MAY: You should watch out for friends like me.

(MAY rests her hand on JODY'S head.)

JODY: Will you? *(yawns)* Will you take me to Alaska? Will you
   build me an igloo? I'm not good at that sort of thing...Can we
   have a Jacuzzi in it...a hot tub thingy...

*(JODY is asleep. MAY takes the drink from JODY'S limp hand and
brushes the veil back from her face.)*

MAY: Yes. Yes. I would probably do almost anything you asked me
   to. Anything. I think that is my destiny. *(beat)* Always the
   bridesmaid. Never the groom.
(She drinks long and deep.)
   I hope they have a bar or two in Inuit land. I'd hate to give up my
   life's work.

BLACKOUT

THE END

Sol

by Lynda Green

Produced by manhattan**theatre**source *in Program B of EstroGenius 2012 with the following cast and crew:*

Director: Rachel Dart

George: John Gardner

June: Kristin Shields*

Sound Designer: Madeleine Gaw

Lighting Designer: R. S. Buck

Stage Manager: Pat Lewis

*Member of Actors' Equity Association

CONTACT
lygreenie@gmail.com

CHARACTERS

GEORGE – 20s - 30s, any race

JUNE – 20s - 30s, any race

Setting: An office in the jungle

Time: Dawn

(Birds and jungle sounds are heard as the predawn sun rises on GEORGE *sitting at a desk in a small office. In the dim light, he has a small desk lamp on, while he cleans and polishes a handgun and fills out corresponding paperwork. There are also two light bulbs fixed to the desk that* GEORGE *occasionally glances at. One is blinking. One is unlit.*

Featured prominently upstage, on the wall, lit on both sides by extra lights, is a large wheel and lever.* Behind the desk, there are shelves holding fruit and canned supplies, an open cabinet, a standing floor fan, and a table with a coffee pot. Stage right are two doors with curtains leading to bedrooms. One has the curtain neatly pulled back and tied. The other is closed. Stage left is a door to outside and a large window with the shutters open. There are additional unseen windows downstage.

As the sun gets brighter, the jungle noises grow louder and the palm trees outside cast long shadows on the office walls. Suddenly, the blinking light on the desk goes out; the second bulb starts flashing red. The lights surrounding the wheel and lever start flashing and an alarm sounds. GEORGE *calmly puts down his work, gets up, pushes his chair in, and walks upstage to turn the giant wheel and pulls the lever. He makes an entry in a file. The sun is fully up. He turns off the desk lamp. He looks around, proud of his work.)*

GEORGE: Gorgeous!

*(*JUNE *enters from the door with the closed curtain. Unlike* GEORGE, *who is in full dress code, with khaki pants, workboots and a t-shirt bearing the name and logo "Sol Solutions,"* JUNE *is wearing shorts and a light sweatshirt and flip flops.)*

GEORGE: Morning, June!

JUNE: Morning, George.

GEORGE: Look at that, will ya? Another beautiful day! A real stunner!

JUNE: Sure is.

GEORGE: That sun. Wow.

* For scaled-back productions, the wheel and level may be amended to a curtained booth-like area, that implies a wheel and lever through sound cues. However, this design must be equally imposing, by being prominently featured and/or backlit, or entirely through sound to convey its importance.

JUNE: Coffee, George?

GEORGE: Nah, that's okay, it'll keep me up all day. Oh, hey—don't use that, that's no good—that's old, let me get you a new cup!

JUNE: This is fine.

GEORGE: No, no—please—allow me! Please.

JUNE: Oh, well okay. Thanks.

GEORGE: It's my pleasure; it is, really, June.

JUNE: Thanks.

GEORGE: Attention! Are you ready for this? Drum roll please!

JUNE: What is that?

GEORGE: I've been working on it during my shifts, during down time. Whole new brewing system—solar-powered. Naturally.

JUNE: You built this? When?

GEORGE: My free time. Check it out—it's quiet, energy efficient; I've gotten the acidity down to almost nothing. Best cup of coffee you'll ever have, guaranteed! Well? What do you think?

JUNE: You're in a good mood this morning.

GEORGE: Why wouldn't it be? It's a beautiful day!

JUNE: Yeah, it is. (*JUNE trips over the cord to the fan, then sits and looks out the window.*) Damn it, does this always have to be right here?

GEORGE: Don't unplug it!!

JUNE: There's no room for anything in this place! I'm sorry. I'm not myself today. (*pause*) I'm so tired.

GEORGE: Long hours. They can get to you.

JUNE: And the heat. Any word from corporate about that third shift?

(*The lights begin to flash again and the alarm sounds.*)

GEORGE: I'll get that one!

(GEORGE pulls the lever and turns the wheel. The alarm and flashing lights stop. He makes a note in the file.)

GEORGE: Will you just look at that sun! I'll never get tired of it! Another great shift! And you're all ready to go. The wheel was a little sticky there for a minute *(GEORGE consults the clipboard)* — at precisely 12:43 a.m. — but I got that taken care of. A little oil, a little love, it shouldn't give you any trouble.

(GEORGE begins putting away the cleaning supplies, and straightening paperwork on the desk. JUNE, vaguely listening, removes her sweatshirt and underneath is wearing a tank top with the Columbia University logo. GEORGE knocks a stack of folders off the desk; momentarily distracted, he forgets the gun on the desk before locking the cabinet.)

GEORGE: Everything's up and running just the way it should be — not a millisecond off-schedule. And of course you can consult my shift report for more detail. Oh, and if you can just double-check my inventory numbers for me, that would be much appreciated. Also, just a head's up: be careful — on your last shift report you had a few missing time entries — you don't want corporate to flag that, but all in all, I am happy to say, the world is still turning, bright and sunny, and all is well! *(looking out the window, with a wink to the sun:)* And I'll see you, sir, tomorrow.

(GEORGE takes a time card out of his pocket and punches out at a clock on the wall — just as JUNE also crosses to the time clock and punches in for her shift.)

GEORGE: June!

JUNE: Yeah?

GEORGE: Aren't you forgetting something? June… Not to be a nag, but aren't you…

JUNE: What?

GEORGE: You can't! Not like that! … You're not in dress code!

JUNE: Yeah, I know. I don't feel like it today.

GEORGE: But you… *(pause)* You have to! It's the rule!

JUNE: I've been thinking about it, and… *(pause)* Can we just forget these rules, George? Nobody's here but us.

GEORGE: I'm just not really comfortable with this. If I'm going to be honest. Which I am.

JUNE: What? Are you going to report me?

GEORGE: No! I mean, of course not—no!

JUNE: Because I'm not going to report you for the false inventory reports you submitted.

GEORGE: That was an honest mistake!

JUNE: An honest mistake that resulted in a whole extra case of peanut butter when we already had a shelf full?

GEORGE: So what? I like peanut butter. Everyone likes peanut butter.

JUNE: I don't.

GEORGE: Happy accident, June! That was an entirely different situation. The fact is you can't clock in like that. What if they see you?

JUNE: Why are whispering? Nobody's going to see me. Nobody's here.

GEORGE: Yes, I understand, but I think it would just behoove you to wear the appropriate, dress-code-approved work clothes because you are a stellar employee and it should be adequately reflected in your attire—and please don't put me in this position!

JUNE: Okay. Fine. Jeez, I'm sorry.

(JUNE exits and returns, wearing a tank top with the company logo.)

GEORGE: Flip flops! I mean, that should be all right. This once.

JUNE: It's so hot already.

GEORGE: Mmm…. Steamy!

JUNE: Why aren't you tired?

GEORGE: *(turning on the fan, speaking very loudly near it)*
I'm glad you asked! It just so happens I've conditioned myself to

not need more than four hours of sleep; it wastes too much of the day. Too much of the day I can use to work!

JUNE: Okay. Great. Well, it is nice to have a little company for a while. And if they ever send out that third shift it would be nice to get out of here for a while and do something with another person.

GEORGE: *(dusting and windexing the desk and coffee area)*
Truly, June? Because I would like that very much. I think that's an excellent suggestion. That, that would be very enjoyable.

JUNE: I hate it here.

GEORGE: What was that? *(pause)* You need a beer? Well, you know, I know it's early in the morning, but a nice cold beer sure does sound like a good idea. Today's going to be a scorcher!

JUNE: I said I hate it here.

GEORGE: Haha, no beer — you're on the job — coffee for you!

JUNE: I just want to go home.

GEORGE: Yes, I agree, the best part is the foam!

JUNE: Forget it.

GEORGE: Will do. Here you are. Coffee: black, one sugar. Guaranteed to perk you up — pun intended!

JUNE: Thanks.

(Two large canvas bags, one right after the other, are dropped from the sky and land just outside the doorway. One is labeled "Sol, Station 32, SUPPLIES." The other is labeled "Sol, Station 32, MAIL.")

JUNE: Mail's here! *(JUNE exits and returns with both bags. She frantically goes through the mailbag, while GEORGE empties the cans from the supply bag.)*

GEORGE: All kidney beans. *(pause)* Alright! Kidney beans! I can do a lot with these. Kidney beans are the best! Just what I wanted!

JUNE: Why are you shouting?

(The lights start flushing; the alarm sounds. JUNE continues sorting the mail.)

GEORGE: Oh, hey, June? June, the alarm is… *(pause)* No worries, I got this one! This one came fast! *(GEORGE turns the wheel; pulls the lever; watches JUNE read a letter.)* June? What's wrong?

JUNE: Our request for a third shift was denied.

GEORGE: Oh. *(pause)* Well, that's disappointing.

JUNE: Disappointing?! They can't do this to us, George! That's just a fact! It's abuse, what they're doing. We need another person down here. It's in our contract. Isn't it in our contract?

GEORGE: No, I don't think it is, actually.

JUNE: It should be. We can't keep doing this. Twelve hour shifts, sun up and sun down, just the two of us. It's impossible. It's inhuman.

GEORGE: I think it's rigorous and challenging and don't you feel strong and accomplished? I know I sure do! You do too; you're just having a bad day. Sometimes even the best workers — like you — have a bad day!

JUNE: George, you're my friend, but seriously, what is wrong with you?

GEORGE: Not a thing! Everything is right with me. Right as rain! Look, June, corporate knows what they're doing. They're very good at making the best decisions for the company. For the world. And I trust them. Whole-heartedly. What's good for the company is good for us! Let's give it another couple of months…

JUNE: Months!

GEORGE: …and put in another scheduling request — before the rainy season starts. You'll see, everything will work out just fine. I've been here for three years — it really gets easier. Don't cry, June. No, really. You shouldn't do that. June? June? Hey, here's something interesting I came across the other day when I was really the monthly newsletter — a little factoid — and I meant to share it with you: did you know that the word "pineapple" is derived from an ancient South American word meaning "excellent fruit"? Which is fortuitous, because here we have one, right here — our very own Excellent Fruit!

JUNE: Pineapple what? Are you kidding me?

GEORGE: Excellent, indeed! That's a pretty obscure fact. It's also a universal symbol of good cheer and hospitality. Whaddya say we pop open a can of this excellent fruit and start this day over.

JUNE: All my mail got returned to me. All my letters.

GEORGE: I'm sorry.

JUNE: Not a single one made it home. And they're all opened! They opened my mail, George — and blacked things out!

GEORGE: Juicy pineapple?

JUNE: I don't want your goddamn juicy pineapple! *(pause)* What am I doing here? George? I can't keep doing this. This job just isn't worth it. *(GEORGE gasps)* I thought this was going to be different. Special. I thought it would be an adventure.

GEORGE: It is special. We are special. That's why you can't write home about it.

JUNE: But why hide it?

GEORGE: We keep the sun in the sky — that's an honor! That's a gift! Don't you think so, June? Don't you?

JUNE: Yeah, I guess.

(Another supply bag is dropped outside; GEORGE *runs to get it.)*

GEORGE: Look — Spanish Limes! Spanish Limes! Isn't that amazing? *(turning away from* JUNE, *towards the fan, whispering:)* Gracias.

JUNE: Why are you thanking me?

GEORGE: What why?

JUNE: Who are you talking to?

GEORGE: No one. You.

JUNE: George…

GEORGE: My apologies. I misspoke.

JUNE: You thanked someone.

GEORGE: No, I didn't. You're hearing things. Because you're overworked and tired.

JUNE: Who are you talking to?

GEORGE: June, I'm very busy, and on second thought, I really do need some sleep, so please, let me finish up and do what I need to around here so I can go. This is technically your shift.

JUNE: George, you know something and you're not telling me and I need to know what *(JUNE trips over the fan's cord, unplugging it)* Seriously, can we move this fan? It doesn't even do anything. George, what are you doing? Get off of me.

GEORGE: Shhhh. This place is bugged! It's in the fan!

JUNE: The what?

GEORGE: They know everything we say! Everything we do! Now quick — plug it back in, plug it back in — there can't be a gap in the tape! *(pause)* What? Why are you just standing there? June, say something.

(JUNE exits and returns with an armful of clothes, which she puts in the empty mailbag. She adds some of the food supplies, and the gun from the desk.)

GEORGE: What are you doing?

JUNE: I quit. I'm done. I'm going home.

GEORGE: You can't do that!

JUNE: I can't do this anymore. I'm sorry to leave you in a bind.

GEORGE: June.

JUNE: George.

GEORGE: There's nowhere for you to go!

JUNE: I'll figure it out.

GEORGE: You can't just walk out into the jungle!

JUNE: I can. You're going to have to contact corporate and tell them…

GEORGE: Listen to me, you can't…

JUNE: … as soon as you can, and ask for a replacement…

GEORGE: …just leave like this!

JUNE: I can't spend one more second in this place. I thought I hated it here and now I know for sure. Corporate's watching us? I can't stay here.

GEORGE: No, I mean, June! Corporate will find you — they won't let you quit! They'll hunt you down in the jungle and drag you back and you'll never be able to break your contract — it's a death sentence! *(pause)* I mean… *(pause)* Never mind.

JUNE: Come again?

GEORGE: Which part, about when, exactly? Pardon?

JUNE: "Death Sentence".

GEORGE: I exaggerate. But it would be… not ideal.

JUNE: You know that for a fact. *(GEORGE nods)* How do you know that?

GEORGE: Just don't go, June. Please.

JUNE: Life is just passing us by here.

GEORGE: No, June, that's not true. You have it all wrong. We are life. The sun rises and sets because of us. The sun, June. To you it may feel like punching a clock and pulling a lever in an office until your contract runs out. I've made my peace with this place because I know that every living creature on this earth breathes and grows and lives because I play my small part from behind this desk. And that that's the closest to God I'll ever get.

JUNE: That's what they want you to think. We don't matter.

GEORGE: Look out of the window — that's your proof.

JUNE: That's not even how it works — I mean physics — the sun doesn't rotate — we do!

GEORGE: I don't need to know the mechanics of it. We don't need to create the miracle. We just stand back and watch.

JUNE: They're lying to us...

GEORGE: To what end? They have no reason...

JUNE: How should I know why? To—to study us! To laugh at us! To keep us busy! Cuz they're bored! Cuz this is just some bullshit job that doesn't mean anything except a tax write off. All I know is I can't stay here anymore. You can't either. We need to go home. You can come with me.

(The alarm sounds; neither of them move.)

GEORGE: Are you really going to ignore that?

JUNE: I am. Don't turn that wheel, George. Don't do it. They're laughing at you.

GEORGE: It's our job. It's what we do.

JUNE: No, it's not.

GEORGE: I am here to do a job!

JUNE: Well, it's my shift and I say we're not doing it.

GEORGE: You abandoned your shift—it's my shift now!

(A warning is sounded over the ringing alarm: "Turn the wheel, Turn the wheel".)

GEORGE: This is ridiculous. I'm not going to let you destroy the entire interplanetary alignment because you're having a bad day.

(JUNE pulls the gun from her bag, turns it on GEORGE.)

JUNE: George, I said no.

GEORGE: Oh, June. Please. Don't do this. Such melodrama.

JUNE: *(JUNE expertly checks and loads the gun)* I mean it, George. I can't spend another day here. And neither can you.

(An emergency countdown begins)

GEORGE: Listen to me. We're both upset. We're exhausted. So I'm just going to walk over here and pull this little lever and turn this little wheel — just this one last time. Then we can figure the rest out.

JUNE: No, George, we're not going to do that! Because it's not real and you're so smart and you're so good, and I hate what they're doing to you.

GEORGE: You're the one with the gun on me, not them. We're running out of time — I'm turning it.

JUNE: Don't you dare.

GEORGE: You're not going to shoot me, June. We both know it

JUNE: I will if I have to. I mean it.

GEORGE: If you do this it will be the end of everything we've ever known!

JUNE: Yeah, I get it; the sun will fall from the sky. Give me another reason!

GEORGE: Because, I love you, and you're ruining everything!

(JUNE drops the gun, which accidentally fires; they both scream. GEORGE, unharmed, runs for the wheel. JUNE tackles him before he reaches it. The alarm suddenly stops. Aside from the sound of birds in the jungle, all is quiet.)

GEORGE: It's finished. Nothing happened. It's all the same. *(pause)* It's all the same. It was all a lie.

JUNE: George, I'm so sorry. Are you hurt?

GEORGE: Nope. I'm quite all right. No harm, no foul. I suppose I'll just mark this one down in the report as 'missed'. And there you go. Back to the drawing board.

(GEORGE sorts through paper work and turns on the desk lamp.)

JUNE: How long ago did you try to leave? How long before they found you?

GEORGE: I don't like talking about that. *(pause)* I was very unhappy for a long time. And I thought I could leave and start over. I was wrong. All you can do is find meaning where you are. Grow where you're planted, and all that. I've learned to love what I do.

And it's been better, recently.

JUNE: George — the lamp.

GEORGE: Yes, I need a lamp, so I can — oh, good lord! I need a lamp!

JUNE: The light! It's getting dark! It's actually getting dark!

GEORGE: Good lord, you broke the sun!

JUNE: I did not break the sun!

GEORGE: You did! You totally broke the sun! *(pause)* It was true!

JUNE: Oh my goodness, oh my goodness, you have to do something! You have to fix it!

GEORGE: It's too late.

JUNE: What are they going to do to us?

GEORGE: We have about an hour head start, I figure.

JUNE: I'm so sorry, George. George?

GEORGE: *(looking around at the bright orange light and growing shadows)* Just look at it.

JUNE: It's beautiful.

GEORGE: It's a miracle.

JUNE: *(quietly)*I did this. I created a miracle.

GEORGE: And I don't love you, by the way. You're my colleague. We're professionals.

JUNE: Well, yeah. Not anymore.

GEORGE: I mean, you're my friend and I care about you. What I'm trying to say is... I don't... not love you.

JUNE: I understand. I don't not love you too, George. *(pause)* So what do we do now?

GEORGE: Whatever we're supposed to.

JUNE: Aren't you worried?

GEORGE: I should be. But I'm not. I'm not at all.

JUNE: Me too. Weird.

GEORGE: Weird indeed.

JUNE: Well, here we go.

(GEORGE *and* JUNE *watch the orange sunset together, with about a foot of distance between them. As the light continues to dim,* JUNE *grabs* GEORGE'S *hand. The lights continue to fade, until only the desk lamp is lit.*)

bLACKOUT

THE END

When Predator Dies

by Catya McMullen

Produced by manhattan**theatre**source *in Program B of EstroGenius 2012 with the following cast and crew:*

Director: DeLisa White

Anabelle: Sheila Joon*

Henry: Jack Reitz

Alexander: David Greenslade

Jacob: Sergio La Dolce

Sound Designer: Madeleine Gaw

Lighting Designer: R. S. Buck

Stage Manager: Pat Lewis

*Member of Actors' Equity Association

CONTACT
McCatya@gmail.com

CHARACTERS
ANABELLE— Painter. She's sweet, a little neurotic. The kind of girl who can help get other people's lives together but never quite completely fix her own. She works multiple part time jobs and has an arsenal of tactics to deal with her anxiety.

HENRY -- A writer. He's got that nice balance of responsibility and humor. Think "grounded bro."

ALEXANDER: The anal retentive roommate. He means well and cares for those around him but has a tight---assed way of showing it. He's methodical. The kind of roommate that leaves passive aggressive notes while also trying to have open communication with his roommates.

JACOB: Frequently has the demeanor of a kid at Disney World. Never quite gets his life together but is okay with it. He's the kind of guy that has never cleaned the bathroom and needs directions every time he does his laundry. He's lovable and seems to get away with it.

Setting: An apartment living room where Gen Y mid 20's live, maybe filled with items from Ikea or various parents' homes. Or maybe they have no furniture and do everything on the carpeted floor.

JACOB, ALEXANDER and HENRY are seated. They are all looking back at the door, nervously, every five seconds.

JACOB: So this is, like, an intervention.

ALEXANDER: I mean...

HENRY: An intervention implies we know what's going on.

ALEXANDER: Well we know she's been-

HENRY: We don't have facts yet.

ALEXANDER: I think the point is that we show her that we're here for her. With...whatever...it is.

HENRY: I hear something.

JACOB: This is an overreaction.

ALEXANDER: Something is clearly going on.

HENRY: Clearly.

ALEXANDER: She's done so much for us.

JACOB: I was sad last week; she made me meatloaf.

ALEXANDER: Which you have yet to do the dishes for.

HENRY: She helped me with a plumbing...issue the other day.

ALEXANDER: She's definitely a valued member of the household.

JACOB: More than that.

ALEXANDER: I hear something.

ANABELLE enters, carrying a few bags. The boys look at her, intently, silently, tensely.

ANABELLE: Hey guys.

HENRY and ALEXANDER: Hello.

ALEXANDER: Take a seat.

HENRY: Have a cookie.

ANABELLE: Everything okay? You just all seem...Jesus, these taste like dog food.

JACOB: Hey!

ALEXANDER: We baked.

HENRY: Wanted you to feel...

ALEXANDER: You doing all right? Everything okay with...everything?

ANABELLE: Fine. Why?

ALEXANDER: Well, we've been...hearing things.

JACOB: And smelling. Don't forget the smell.

ANABELLE: What?

HENRY: What is going on with you?

ALEXANDER: The walls aren't that thin. And we've been hearing things at night.

JACOB: Weird things. I mean, either you're torturing a banshee or nursing some injured yack-

HENRY: Those are the options?

ALEXANDER: Or, you're weeping. Nightly. The point is; we're concerned.

HENRY: He's concerned. I tried to explain to him that you're probably just going through a phase.

ANABELLE: A phase?

HENRY: And that this was none of our business and-

ANABELLE: You guys-

ALEXANDER: But it's not just the noises...it's the stench, too.

ANABELLE: What stench?

ALEXANDER: Coming from your room...

JACOB: It smells like nursing home and feet.

ANABELLE: What?

ALEXANDER: No, it doesn't.

HENRY: He's exaggerating.

JACOB: It wafts.

ALEXANDER: And finally, we decided-

HENRY: He decided-

ALEXANDER: To take a peak in your room-

ANABELLE: You went in my room?

ALEXANDER: And we found this...

He takes out a large shopping bag filled with onions. They spill over and roll around the stage.

JACOB: And that's when we realized things had gotten kinda weird, you know?

ANABELLE: You had no right to go in my room-

ALEXANDER: We're worried. What's going on?

JACOB: Is it witchcraft?

ANABELLE: What?

HENRY: Jacob.

JACOB: Ancient ritual? A new exfoliating recipe?

ANABELLE: No. It's just-

JACOB: Because your pores are fine.

ALEXANDER: You can talk to us.

HENRY: She's trying to.

ANABELLE: It's dumb.

JACOB: Can't be as dumb as the time I masturbated with Tabasco sauce.

HENRY: What?

ANABELLE: I've been cutting-

ALEXANDER: Yourself?

ANABELLE: No! Forget it.

JACOB: This is a safe space. Share with us.

HENRY: You don't have to.

ANABELLE: You guys are going to think I'm insane.

JACOB: Already do.

ALEXANDER: Jacob! I mean it's been really uncomfortable to live with. I feel compromised-

HENRY: We just want to know you're okay.

ALEXANDER: I want to know what's going on. Listen, I have the emergency contact information you gave me with the sublet agreement. I can contact your mother if-

ANABELLE: No, don't do that.

ALEXANDER: If you're cutting yourself, this might be outside of what we can all handle.

ANABELLE: I'm not-you don't understand.

ALEXANDER: If you need assistance-

ANABELLE: She overreacts to everything. She'll think something's actually wrong and will show up here or call me 70 times a day because of nothing-

ALEXANDER: You might need help outside the scope of our abilities-

ANABELLE: Onions. I cut the onions. To cry.

ALEXANDER: That's-

HENRY: Genius.

ANABELLE: It's become this nightly ritual.

ALEXANDER: When did you start this?

ANABELLE: A few weeks ago.

ALEXANDER: Why?

ANABELLE: I don't know, I like how it feels. I've been having kind of a weird time recently.

ALEXANDER: That onions fix?

ANABELLE: You're going to think it's stupid.

JACOB: We support you.

HENRY: Yeah, come on. It's us-

ALEXANDER: I'm just glad you're not in danger.

JACOB: Tellll usssss.

ANABELLE: It started the night I went to that stupid party Tino threw. The walls were covered in canvas and there were paint brushes everywhere and this beautiful acrylic paint. There's something about the smell of it. It's always made me feel kind of tingly and inspired. And I was whiffing it and trying to not look like I was huffing paint and I looked around the room and there were all of these semi famous people just, like, on the spot making these lovely or weird images on the walls and I was just there, in my corner, for forty-five minutes, holding my paint brush, afraid to pick a color to begin with. I kept thinking isn't this supposed to be what I do? Isn't this supposed to be who I am? It used to be that I would just feel this warmth and the image would be there and my hands would know what to do and this feeling inside of me would be in the painting and people would show up and see it and then they get to have this experience of their own inner life. Sometimes I feel like it's why I was born. Because there's something kind of profound about being alive, you know? But recently it's been so hard. There are so many standards and so many stages of people to tell me what's good and what isn't. It's like every time I paint, I have to be good. I have to prove myself as an artist, or whatever. And it's like art is trying and failing and failing better but there just isn't enough time in this city. I feel like I'm always ten steps behind where I should be and then I get more blocked and more broke and then freeze up and nothing works and then I get so wrapped up in the social politics of being an artist in New York that I suddenly feel like I can't access the thing that drives me to want to do it.

After a pause.

ALEXANDER: Maybe it's time to pursue another career or another city-

HENRY: Dude.

JACOB: Don't move!

HENRY: You just have to keep going. I have the same thing with writing. It gets easier.

ANABELLE: I know. It's just annoying. Because when I don't paint, I kind of freeze up and my life goes grey and I want to punch people and don't feel like myself.

HENRY: Yeah.

ANABELLE: It's kind of this bind I'm in.

ALEXANDER: I still don't get where the onions fall into this.

ANABELLE: Oh, right, sorry. So I come home after the party. And I'm sitting in my room, staring at my walls, missing that feeling of inspiration or whatever. I wasn't even worked up. I was just kind of flat. And then I realize how hungry I am and how much I just want a fucking frittata I start ferociously cooking. It's like 2 am and I'm chopping veggies and I chop and I chop and I chop and my head is super loud and so I turn on the TV and *Independence Day* is on. And Will Smith is being a bad ass and Randy Quaid is all drunk and just as I start to slice the onions Bill Pullman gives this, like, world saving speech-

JACOB: Oh hell yes-

ANABELLE: -And the fumes hit my eyes and I just started blubbering. I wept so hard, it was like a vitamin B12 shot for my emotional

life. And the next night, I just found myself turning on TNT and doing the same thing.

HENRY: What movie was it this time?

ANABELLE: *Cast Away.*

JACOB: Oh, Wilson.

ANABELLE: I've been doing it every night since. With or without TV.

JACOB: Whoa.

ANABELLE: I've never felt better.

ALEXANDER: It just doesn't seem right.

ANABELLE: And I've been painting. Look.

ANABELLE pulls out two paintings of her satchel. They are fiery, soulful and beautiful images.

HENRY: Can we try it?

ANABELLE: You don't think it's weird?

JACOB: It's completely weird. Let's get our cry on.

ALEXANDER: I don't know.

ANABELLE gets four onions out of the shopping bags and four knives. ANABELLE, HENRY and JACOB sit in a circle each take an onion and start slicing them through the rest of the scene, crying progressively more and more. They cut them into bits. They hold them up to their eyes. Maybe they chop multiple onions. ALEXANDER watches them. He paces around them.

JACOB: Awesome.

HENRY: So what do we do?

ALEXANDER: I can't believe you all. This is just-

ANABELLE: Chop and feel, my friends.

ALEXANDER: So...

JACOB: But what do we feel? Oh God that burns.

ANABELLE: Alexander, join us.

ALEXANDER: No. Thank you.

HENRY: Come on, man. It's catharsis.

ALEXANDER: It's peculiar. I don't need catharsis.

JACOB: Once you get over the pain of the stinging, it feels kind of good.

ANABELLE: What's a moment you wish you could re-feel, right now?

JACOB: When Predator dies.

ALEXANDER: Oh, come on.

HENRY: That was sad.

JACOB: Not as sad as when Mufasa died.

HENRY: Or every minute of *Finding Neverland*.

They cry harder.

ALEXANDER: I'm uncomfortable.

JACOB: *E.T.*

HENRY: *Elf.*

ALEXANDER: The Will Ferrell movie?

HENRY: When Santa's sleigh gets enough Christmas spirit power to miss running over all of those spontaneous carolers? So moving.

ALEXANDER *inconspicuously, slowly sits down. He watches them but doesn't participate.*

ANABELLE: What about moments not captured in cinematic history?

They look at each other, HENRY *and* JACOB *don't have answers until-*

ALEXANDER: The first time I saw the Sagrada Familia.

JACOB: The what?

ALEXANDER: Barcelonian Cathedral.

HENRY: Seriously?

ANABELLE: No judgment.

ALEXANDER: It's beautiful.

ANABELLE: Giovanni Bellini's *Ecstasy of St. Francis.*

ALEXANDER hides his face, starting to cry progressively more throughout. They don't notice.

JACOB: Breast reductions.

HENRY: The first time I read *As I Lay Dying.*

JACOB: This time I saw this dog get run over by a car in a crosswalk on 53rd and Lex.

HENRY: That's so sad.

JACOB: *(weeping)* And why I don't jaywalk.

HENRY: Babies.

JACOB: Starving ones or regular ones?

HENRY: *(sobbing)*Both.

ANABELLE: Sunsets.

JACOB: They make you sad?

ANABELLE: They're pretty. *(beat)* Jack Franlor. Broke my heart.

The mood starts to become serious.

HENRY: Casey leaving.

ANABELLE: My childhood dog, Tiny, dying.

JACOB: My grandpa Nick dying.

HENRY: My father dying.

ALEXANDER is weeping profusely.

ANABELLE: You guys...*(To ALEXANDER)* What is it?

After a moment.

ALEXANDER: I don't know...

Then, another pause.

ANABELLE: Yeah.

THE END

Books Not Now

by Kira Lauren

Produced by manhattan**theatre**source *in Program C of EstroGenius 2012 with the following cast and crew:*

Director: Sharon Hunter

Him: John Say*

Her: Kate Dulcich

Sound Designer: Earline Stephen

Lighting Designer: Daisy Long

Stage Manager: Earline Stephen

*Member of Actors' Equity Association

CONTACT
kiralauren@gmail.com

CHARACTERS
HIM — Man, early thirties

HER — Woman, early thirties

A man and a woman in their early thirties are sitting on the floor surrounded by books. She is sorting through them his is placing them into three separate piles according to HER *instructions.* HER *instructions take on a rhythmic flow....*

HER: Books now...books not now....Goodwill....books now...books notnow....books now.... Goodwill.....books not now.....books now...booksnotnow...booksnow....

HIM:: Do let me know if you find one of mine in there.

HER: That's doubtful. Books now...books now...books not now....

HIM: Yes, doubtful...*(Stung, he looks around for ammunition)...(disparagingly)* "Hypnotize Yourself Thin"?

HER: *(She looks up)* That's yours.

HIM: *(He realizes this is true)* Oh...yes.

HER: Books now...books now...books not now....

HIM: ...Remind me again what "books not now" means?

HER: Storage. Books now...booksnotnow...booksnotnow....books –

HIM: *(Interrupting)* This one is mine.

HER: *(She looks up)* <u>A Prayer for Owen Meany</u>? Since when is that yours?

HIM: I love this book! It's my favourite.

HER: You mean of the three books you've read?

HIM: Yes, of the three books I've read, this one happens to be my favourite.

HER: Well, even if that were true, which I doubt, it also happens to be my favourite. And since the chances of you actually having not only read it, but also loved it, are small, I'm going to say that I get to keep it.

HIM: Can't you buy a new copy?

HER: Can't you?

(Pause)

HER: Oh fine.

(He gently places the book to one side)

HER: Books now...booksnotnow...booksnotnow....books- Ah.

(Pause...she holds the book up)

HIM: *(He leans in to read the cover)* "7 Ways to Maintain a Lifelong Happy Marriage". Mmm.

HER: Goodwill.

HIM: Really? Goodwill?

HER: Well, it isn't a "books now" is it?

HIM: No. I guess not. Do you plan to pull it out of storage later?

HER: No....maybe....I don't know. (Pause). What would you think if you walked into Goodwill and saw this on the shelf? Would you think the person who donated it has a successful marriage and felt they should spread the "happiness"? Or would you think that the marriage was over and the book had been a waste of time?

HIM: Why?

HER: I wouldn't like to give the wrong impression.

HIM: Oh Jesus.

HER: What? I don't want to be responsible for misleading some poor person looking for a way to save their marriage. I couldn't stand the thought of someone walking into Goodwill, picking up this book, and thinking it was coming from a home that sets some sort of example of what a marriage should be.

HIM: No one is going to think that

HER: *(Continuing over HIM)* Nor do I like the idea that this book could actually be broadcasting our failure to the world.

HIM: I think we already may have done that -

HER: This book - this tiny little book - the contents of which is supposed to single-handedly safeguard a marriage –

HIM: Hey, it's just a book

HER: *(Getting worked up)* Is it? Is it?

HIM: Yes. It's a book. A tiny little book. He's probably secretly divorced.

HER: He spent 25 years following the same 10 couples, or something like that.

HIM: 25 years....so no pressure there then for them to stay together.

HER: Not all of them stayed together.

HIM: Well, then, there you have it.

HER: What's that supposed to mean?

HIM: It means he's full of shit.

HER: That's ridiculous. You can't make a blanket statement like that.

HIM: Why not? Books like these are all the same. Someone's Personal opinions about bla bla bla. I should write one. 7 Ways to a Better Night's Sleep. 1. Go to bed earlier. 2. Wake up later. 3. –

HER: No one would buy that book.

HIM: Are you kidding me? I bet it already exists and has sold a million copies. *(He pulls out his iphone and begins typing, looking for the book online, he continues to do so as he speaks).* Those kinds of books are a dime a dozen. Take a major problem that exists in the world, come up with 7 totally obvious ways to deal with it and BAM – you have a national bestseller. I mean, what do you think the 4 billion diet books in Barnes and Noble have in common? 1. Don't put shit in your mouth. 2.Get up off the couch and take a walk. 3. The End – Ah! Here's one...."71 ways to a Better Night's Sleep". 71....hmm. Well, that might take a bit more time to write....*(he continues reading his phone).*

HER: Wow. *(She takes* HIM *in and quietly starts to cry).*

HIM: *(Not hearing HER)* Oh, here's an even better one...."Eat Your Way to Better Night's Sleep". Well that one kills two birds with one stone, doesn't it? *(He finally looks up and sees HER crying)*. What? What have I said now?

HER: Nothing. Nothing.

(He accepts this, which infuriates HER)

HER: Ok then....if these books are so goddamn easy to write, where can I find yours? On which shelf of Barnes and Noble would that be?

HIM: Now you're being ridiculous.

HER: Am I? Am I? Because if you are going to so easily dismiss this book -this tiny little book – on the grounds that any asshole could write it, then I'd like to know where yours is?

(He thinks about this for a moment.)

HIM: You know where mine is?

(She glares at HIM)

HIM: It's right here. *(He taps his head)*

HER: Oh my god.

(She makes an exasperated gesture and then returns to sorting books. As she does this, mumbling booksnow, booksnotnow, Goodwill under HER breath, He begins to flip through the marriage book. There is a pause as he does this and she sorts.)

HIM: You know what I think?

HER: What?

HIM: What I really think?

HER: What?

HIM: I think...maybe we should have read it.

HER: I did read it! Are you fucking kidding me? I did read it! I tried everything in this book. I tried *(she starts flipping through the book to find the right chapter)* "Learn your partner's daily routines so you can ask about them at night". I tried *(flipping to a different section)* "Ask About Your Partners Life Goals". We took the quiz at the back, remember? You rolled your eyes through the whole thing and gave Disney characters as half your answers. Goddammit! "Maybe we should have read it". Maybe YOU should have read it!

Silence as he takes this in.

HIM: Would it have helped?

She angers and he cuts HER off before she blows

HIM: Wait, hear me out. I'm not attacking you...I'm asking you honestly. Would it have helped? Do you think that every couple out there who read this book isn't in the middle of a divorce right now?

HER: No. Of course not.

HIM: We're surrounded by books like these but they aren't achieving anything. The divorce rate is skyrocketing, the whole country is obese despite those 4 million diet books. Everywhere we look there are solutions but that doesn't seem to be changing the problem. Knowledge, it would seem, isn't always power.

HER: No. It's not. But it is a tool. What you do with that tool is what matters. That's the point. You can read "Don't put shit in your mouth" over and over again but you have to actually not put shit in your mouth in order to lose weight. That's all I ever expected of you.

HIM: To not put shit in my mouth?

HER: Actually, I'd have preferred it if you kept your bullshit in your mouth.

HIM: And my dumb jokes too.

(This softens her)

HER: Yes. And your dumb jokes at totally inappropriate times.

(They share a small smile. She goes back to sorting through the books. He helps her for a moment and then tentatively decides to share.)

HIM: I still love you, you know. This isn't my choice, this isn't what I want for us.

HER: *(Gently at first)* How is this not your choice? You may not have said it out loud but you chose this every day. Every time I needed to talk about how I felt and you dismissed me.....how did you not choose this?

HIM: And here we go again. Look, I'm sorry that I don't understand the way you wanted to deal with things. It's just not my way.

HER: I didn't need you to understand! Don't you get it? It doesn't have to be your way for you to support mine. To be here for mine. To listen to mine. You don't have to understand or agree, even, but you were my partner. I chose you. That means you have to show up.

HIM: I showed up.

HER: Did you? Really?

(Silence)

HER: I was at work one day, sitting at my desk, staring out the window and I overhear Alex in the cubicle next to me bitching to Doug about his wife and how she's made him read this stupid book about loss because she's just had her third miscarriage and she just can't seem to find a way through. He's complaining about the book but underneath it there is this softness...this gentle appreciation that she is surviving by reading a book that is going to give her the answers on moving forward, on waking up in the morning and actually getting out of bed. And so even though he's a man and he's supposed to be seen to despise this kind of thing, you can tell that he doesn't. Not because he liked the book, but because he loves his wife. He loves her so much and grieves with her so deeply that he didn't mind reading a stupid book if it gives her any kind of comfort in what they will probably look back on as the worst time of their life. *(Pause)* And I had to get out of there. I got up and barely made it to the bathroom in time to throw up in the sink. And I stood there for a moment staring at myself in the mirror, wondering if I should tell Alex that I understand, that I've read that stupid book myself. But we're not supposed to talk about these things. Not really. We can bitch about a book, we can laugh at the idea that it could get us through something horrible but we aren't supposed to say just how horrible it really is. We aren't supposed to struggle or suffer or admit to being "not ok". And so I walk back to my desk and keep working. And later, when Alex asks me how my weekend was, I say "it was great, thanks" and smile. And he smiles and says the same. *(Pause)* I could keep that front up at work, but I just couldn't do it at home. I just couldn't.

HIM: *(He crosses to the copy of Owen Meany and picks it up).* Do you know why I read this book? Do you know how it happens to be my favourite of the three books I've ever read?

HER: No. I'm still having trouble believing that you have actually read it.

HIM: Well, I did. I read it because you loved it so much. I kept thinking of you on our honeymoon, weeping over this book, talking about it over dinner, your hands up near your face in that way you gesture when you're excited. You were so happy then, you glowed. And I thought, if I can just help you recapture some of that...if I can give you a little of that back...then maybe, maybe we can move forward. Maybe we would be ok. So I read it. Secretly, after you went to bed, when you were out with friends, at my lunch hour at work. And one night I come home, and I've finished the book, and I can't wait to tell you. I can't wait to tell you that I gasped out loud in the same place you did at the end. And I walk in the door and you're gone. Just gone. No note, no forewarning, just all your stuff gone and some dirty dishes in the sink.

HER: I meant to clean those. I felt terrible when I remembered that I hadn't.

HIM: Yes, well.

(Pause)

HER: Thank you. For reading it. For wanting those things for me.

He reaches out and touches her, maybe he takes HER hand. A small moment.

HER: Shall we?

HIM: Sure.

She begins sorting again...."Books Now....books not now...books not now....books not now...".

Lights Fade.

THE END

Life on Mars

by Trish Cole

Produced by manhattan**theatre**source *in Program C of EstroGenius 2012 with the following cast and crew:*

Director: Sara Lyons

Male Cop: Patrick Walsh*

Lesbian Fugitive: Marcie Henderson*

Female Reporter: Libby Collins*

Sound Designer: Earline Stephen

Lighting Designer: Daisy Long

Stage Manager: Earlene Stephen

CONTACT
tcole84@hotmail.com

CHARACTERS

MALE COP

LESBIAN FUGITIVE– wearing an orange jumpsuit.

FEMALE REPORTER -- wearing a trench coat and a security badge.

Setting: A secure airport concourse in the future.

Life on Mars is a campy, futuristic drama about the final ten minutes a lesbian fugitive spends on Earth. As she waits in shackles to board the last penal transport to Mars, the fugitive buoys the loss of home, of Earth forever, through purpose.

At rise: An airport concourse waiting lounge. A single row of chairs. Chains rattle.

(COP enters, sweeping the room with his drawn gun. FUGITIVE, in shackles, is dragged behind him by the chain at her waist.)

COP: Clear!

FUGITIVE: Take it easy. The chains are ... hard to negotiate.

COP: *(Holstering his weapon.)* Poor you.

FUGITIVE: It's not necessary. Your commando attitude. The chains. The gun. The Taser.

COP: It's my job to do three things today: keep you alive; keep you from escaping; and get you on that last penal transport to Mars. Now sit down.

(COP pushes FUGITIVE down into the middle chair.)

FUGITIVE: Don't forget about the press interview.

COP: Your celebrity status is not mission critical.

FUGITIVE: It's the last chance I'll ever have to set the story, to secure the immortality, of my people.

COP: Three things. Alive. Secure. Goodbye.

FUGITIVE: I'm leaving. I'm chained. And no one is going to kill me.

COP: The term is "assassinate." There's a bounty on your head. The last lesbian on Earth.

FUGITIVE: I'm like a unicorn.

COP: There are plenty of people who'd like a unicorn head mounted on their library wall.

FUGITIVE: Are you one of them?

COP: Like I said, I have my orders. Nothing else matters.

FUGITIVE: Some things matter. Human things.

COP: Hey, shut it. I don't care. Save it for the reporter.

FUGITIVE: Where is she?

COP: I don't know.

FUGITIVE: Can you at least take these chains off for the interview?

COP: No.

FUGITIVE: I'm not going to run.

COP: That's what they all say.

FUGITIVE: I want to go.

COP: To Mars.

FUGITIVE: Yeah. It's where my people are.

COP: Only because we put them there. Forcibly.

FUGITIVE: They say it's a land of purity and innocence, a land where...

COP: ...what?

FUGITIVE: ...where the sun sets red every night. Blood orange across the sky.

COP: It's a penal colony.

FUGITIVE: It's a planet. Of all lesbians.

COP: Genetic outlaws.

FUGITIVE: A beautiful planet.

COP: A prison planet.

FUGITIVE: God, people like you. You know? I'm so over Earth.

COP: Hey, if I had it my way—and if we had enough fuel—I'd send you to Pluto.

FUGITIVE: So you are one of them?

COP: I told you. Three things. Nothing more. Nothing less. I have my orders.

FUGITIVE: But do you believe? In your heart where your humanness lives and breathes?

COP: It doesn't matter what I believe.

FUGITIVE: I was born here.

COP: A deviant.

FUGITIVE: Human. We have that in common—you know? We share that much.

COP: You should have opted for genetic altering when you had your chance.

FUGITIVE: These lungs—right? They were made for …*(Takes a deep breath.)*…air.

COP: *(Instinctively breathes.)* I thought you wanted to go.

FUGITIVE: I do.

COP: Is that why they found you hiding under the kitchen floorboards of some Quakers farming syrup in Vermont? After five years on the run?

FUGITIVE: I like syrup. Not everything is about politics.

(Beat)

FUGITIVE: My wife altered.

COP: Geez, you had a wife?

FUGITIVE: We married when it used to be legal. She was a teacher. Tall. Auburn hair. Long fingered, long toes, long everything. She had this tiny scar on her left cheek.

COP: What happened to her?

FUGITIVE: Like I said. She altered.

(The REPORTER enters in a swoop of trench coat. COP draws his gun.)

COP: Freeze!

(FUGITIVE cowers.)

REPORTER: *(With her hands in the air.)* I'm the reporter. I have a security pass. It's around my neck.

COP: Let me see it.

(She holds it up. COP lowers his weapon. FUGITIVE recovers.)

FUGITIVE: About time.

COP: Your interviewee's due in the transport pod in about ten minutes. The technicians need to hibernate her for the journey.

REPORTER: Security was rather thorough…. How much time?

COP: Ten minutes.

REPORTER: *(Her hand moves into her pocket, a compulsion, feels for the hidden object, finds it.)* Ten minutes.

FUGITIVE: Ten minutes.

REPORTER: *(Approaches FUGITIVE. Sticks out her hand.)* Hi, I'm from the Hourly Tribune. Jessica Mears.

(They shake. Chains rattle.)

FUGITIVE: I'm…

REPORTER: …the last living lesbian on Earth. I know. Shall we start?

(Pulls a digital voice recorder from her pocket.)

(COP reactively pulls his gun.)

FUGITIVE: Uh…I…

REPORTER: *(Waving the recorder at COP to prove its harmlessness.)* We don't have much time. So, you think you were born this way? Can a genetic predisposition be a criminal act?

COP: *(Holstering gun.)* Carry on.

FUGITIVE: I uhh…

REPORTER: What's your stance on infant DNA altering to restructure sexual orientation?

FUGITIVE: I want to answer to something meaningful.

REPORTER: Meaningful?

FUGITIVE: These are my final ten minutes on Earth. I am about to board the last penal, the last anything, transport to Mars. I'm leaving home. This is it. I want human questions — not lesbian, not politics — just human. One Earthling to another.

REPORTER: I don't understand.

FUGITIVE: I'm never going to taste a lemon again. A lemon. Wrap your mind around that.

REPORTER: We're wasting valuable time.

COP: It's always the same with these radical intergalactic lesbian fugitives. They over-process everything.

FUGITIVE: Blueberries.

REPORTER: *(To COP)* Can we have the room for five minutes? Some privacy might be more conducive to getting the story here.

COP: Absolutely not.

REPORTER: This interview is for the government archives. All I'm getting here is fruit.

COP: She's a shy little unicorn. Take a corner.

(REPORTER pulls FUGITIVE to her feet and guides her to a corner where they speak out of hearing distance of COP.)

FUGITIVE: Christ. I thought you'd never make it. What happened?

REPORTER: It's not important.

FUGITIVE: Perhaps. Do you have the package?

REPORTER: *(Indicating the voice recorder.)* It's in here.

FUGITIVE: So...?

REPORTER: What?

FUGITIVE: How do I know that's not a virus in there? What's your plan? Infect me so I land on Mars and wipe out the little of what's left of lesbians in the entire universe?

REPORTER: Oh that!

FUGITIVE: Yes, that.

REPORTER: *(Clears her throat.)* Two three-legged poodles met four dachshunds on the seventh moon of Venus.

FUGITIVE: Okay. The code is good. Hand it over.

(REPORTER opens the battery compartment of the recorder and hands over a vial. FUGITIVE tucks it into her shoe/waistband/pocket.)

REPORTER: May I ask one thing?

FUGITIVE: I meant what I said about the lemons.

REPORTER: No, it's not that. What's in the vial?

FUGITIVE: You don't know?

REPORTER: They said it's best if I don't.

FUGITIVE: Life on Mars.

REPORTER: I don't get it.

FUGITIVE: We know Earth is going to sever all ties with the colony. We're on our own after today. I'm going to get into the space pod, with this vial hidden, the technicians will set our autopilot course, and the two of us, me and the future, this vial, will hibernate our way to Mars.

REPORTER: I know it's important—but what is it?

FUGITIVE: A penal colony. Lesbians. All women. Here on Earth, the lesbian gene has been eradicated. It's the end of the line for us. In another fifty years, when the last of us die off on Mars, lesbians will be gone completely from the universe.

REPORTER: Offspring.

FUGITIVE: Bingo.

REPORTER: You mean that's…ewww.

FUGITIVE: A genetic hodgepodge.

REPORTER: The Garden of Eden. On Mars.

FUGITIVE: With thirty-seven different guys — and no snake.

(An INTERCOM announcement interrupts.)

INTERCOM: *(OS)* Department of Planetary Corrections pod flight #2762. Now boarding. Technicians are standing by.

COP: *(From across the room)* That's us. Ma'am, time for you to go. I have to escort the fugitive to the pod bay.

(REPORTER gathers herself and heads toward the door.)

FUGITIVE: Hey, reporter. Let me ask you something. Why did you...want this story?

REPORTER: Well, there was this one time in college. I was drunk — but it was wonderful.

(REPORTER exits.)

COP: Let's go.

FUGITIVE: Has it been ten minutes already?

COP: I thought you wanted to go.

(COP takes FUGITIVE by the shackles to escort her.)

FUGITIVE: I do. *(Urgency creeps into her voice.)* Will you do me a favor? Please?

COP: Probably not.

FUGITIVE: It's my wife. Find her. Say goodbye for me. Tell her I...I.... Tell her.

COP: I can't.

FUGITIVE: She's married — to a man — lives in Japan, in a town called Kochi. Has a kid. Can you find her? She's tall. Auburn hair.

(She touches her left cheek at the memory of her wife's scar.)

(COP leads FUGITIVE toward the gangway.)

COP: It's against protocol.

FUGITIVE: Do they remember? The ones who altered?

COP: Sorry.

FUGITIVE: We met in Vermont. She worked at a B&B in the kitchen. I fell in love with her blueberry pancakes.

(She puts her shackled hands on the forearm of COP, who stops.)

Do you think it's true? About the sunsets? On Mars?

COP: I'm no scientist.

FUGITIVE: Red. Every night. Blood orange across the sky.

(FUGITIVE takes one last deep breath into her lungs.)

(They exit into the gangway.)

(Lights out.)

THE END

Bazookas

by Sharon Goldner

Produced by manhattan**theatre**source *in Program C of EstroGenius 2012 with the following cast and crew:*

Director: Olivia Kinter

Woman: Yvonne Gougelet*

Boob 1: MaryLynn Suchan

Boob 2: Sabrina Blackburn

Sound Designer: Earline Stephen

Lighting Designer: Daisy Long

Stage Manager: Earlene Stephen

*Member of Actors' Equity Association

CONTACT
shargoldner@comcast.net

CHARACTERS
WOMAN—20s-30s; should be somewhat small-breasted

BOOB 1 & BOOB 2—both boobs should wear their hair in buns piled atop their heads so they look like nipples

Setting: WOMAN enters "dressing room" of a store carrying clothes to try on. She takes off her top and holds various clothes up against her chest in bra, but is dissatisfied with each outfit's potential. BOOBS enter.

WOMAN: I want to talk about my boobs. I took them out so you could see. Here's Boob 1 *(indicating BOOB 1)* and here's Boob 2 *(indicating BOOB 2)*

BOOB 1: I want to have a real name.

WOMAN: No names.

BOOB 2: We could be Ben and Jerry.

BOOB 1: We could be Bert and Ernie.

WOMAN: No names.

BOOB 1: We could be The Jugs.

BOOB 2: Sounds like a country group.

WOMAN: They always do this, my boobs. Things tend to get a little out of hand when I set them free. Listen you two: do you want to go back in the bra? Do you? I'll get the underwire, I swear I will. *(they calm down)* There. That's better.

(a beat, then)

BOOB 1: Tah-tahs.

BOOB 2: Hooters.

BOOB 1: Chesticles.

BOOB 2: Sounds like a popsicle tit frozen on a stick.

WOMAN: Something's wrong with my boobs.

BOOB 1 & 2: We resent that.

WOMAN: My mother said the place in-between the breasts is called a valley. I'm not making this up. She also called them bosom. A bosom has a valley.

BOOB 1: That's what it was called back in the day. You had a bosom. No one says bosom anymore. It's gone the way of archaic words. Bosom might as well be Latin for boobs.

WOMAN: Well, whatever language it's in --- I don't have a valley. Call it urban blight. Call it the decay of our cities. Call it missing in action.

BOOB 2: They don't call it a valley anymore either. That's Latin for cleavage.

WOMAN: The thing is --- I've got one boob over here (indicating #1; #1 waves) and I've got one over here *(indicating #2; #2 curtsies)*. Waaaay over here. And there's a separation in-between. It's like I've got the Midwestern Plains --- nothing but flatlands for miles and miles as far as the eye can see. And the female eye, it's always 20/20 when it comes to boobs. I wish I could say it wasn't always this way *(tries it out)*. It WASN'T always this way. It wasn't always THIS WAY.

BOOB 1: It was always this way.

BOOB 2: Trust us.

WOMAN: I don't know exactly what happened. We all start out the same.

BOOB 2: All little girls are born the same way.

BOOB 1: We aren't present in the original packaging.

BOOB 2: Little boys, little girls, we're all indistinguishable from one another.

WOMAN: Two little brown dots. Nipples. I didn't really think much of them. Not in the beginning anyway.

BOOB 1: I know we didn't.

BOOB 2: Those were good times.

WOMAN: All the girls at my elementary school started to develop in the 5th grade. We left for summer vacation at the end of 4th grade flat-chested, and three months later when school started again, some of the girls came back to class with boobs. Out and out boobs.

BOOB 1: Big mommas.

WOMAN: Other girls had breast buds --- little pokes in their shirts.

BOOB 2: Booblings.

WOMAN: I had nothing. *(looks at the breasts)* I said NOTHING.

BOOB 1: Hey --- don't take it out on us.

BOOB 2: Breasts have feelings too, you know.

WOMAN: Ten years old and those girls had boobs. I'm talking your mother's boobs. I went up to a friend, Wendy Goldblatt. "Hey Wendy," I said. "Wow. So, how was your summer?"

BOOB 1: She went to the ocean.

BOOB 2: Worked with old people at the senior center.

BOOB 1: And animals at the animal shelter.

BOOB 2: Wendy Goldblatt --- what an all-around great gal.

BOOB 1: I'm thinking --- .

BOOB 2: Me too! And are you thinking what I'm thinking?

(a beat)

BOOB 1: Yup, yup. Same thought.

WOMAN: How do you know you're both thinking the same thought?!

BOOB 2: Boob telepathy.

WOMAN: Oh for Christ's sake.

BOOB 1: Remember when she prayed and prayed for boobs?

BOOB 2: *(mocking)* Oh please God, please. I'll never ask for another thing as long as I live.

BOOB 1: People always say that. But they never really mean it.

WOMAN: So I asked God for some boobs. I was 10 years old.

BOOB 1: The really stunning 10 year olds are asking for world peace.

BOOB 2: Or an end to homelessness.

WOMAN: I wanted to start off small --- decorating my little world

First, and then, moving on to bigger and better things. I would have asked for world peace; I just thought I'd plead a better case *(sheepish)* if I had boobs first is all. *(a beat)* I don't want to talk about this. I want to talk about Wendy Fucking Goldblatt.

BOOB 1: What an unusual middle name.

BOOB 2: Is it a family name? The Fucking's from Baltimore by way of Eastern Europe?

WOMAN: I wanted to know where Wendy Goldblatt got her boobs from. Is that too much to ask? It's supposed to be a good thing, this asking questions thing. How else are you supposed to learn?

BOOB 1: And what did she say, this Wendy Fucking Goldblatt with the big boobs?

BOOB 2: I wish I had been there to hear it first-hand.

WOMAN: Well --- you weren't there; you were nowhere in sight! You wanna know what she said? You know what Wendy fucking Goldblatt said to me?!

BOOB 1: I dunno.

BOOB 2: Me either.

WOMAN: That's EXACTLY what she said --- "I DUNNO." She didn't know what happened. How can you not know? That's what I asked Wendy Goldblatt. Hello, you had to notice something was going on. You had to realize that you had DEVELOPED! Land developers had come in the middle of the night, surveying the chest land, deeming it suitable to build breasts on. A double-decker mall, that's what you got, and I want one too. Please, Wendy, please!

BOOB 1: Begging is never the way to go.

BOOB 2: It wreaks of desperation --- a sad, pathetic smell.

BOOB 1: Hold your nose.

BOOB 2: Believe me, if I had one, I would.

WOMAN: Wendy Goldblatt said I was crazy. She wouldn't tell me the secret. I can't be friends with someone who doesn't share.

BOOB 1: All this talk about us. They're at the forefront of everybody's mind.

BOOB 2: What about men? I thought their penises were.

WOMAN: Remember that boy who wrote a poem about you two?

BOOB 1: Really? We were but wee little --- littler --- things then.

BOOB 2: I'm impressed. Recite it, recite it.

WOMAN: *(clears throat)* Roses are red; Violets are blue; Sidewalks are flat; And so are you.

BOOB 1: Oh my.

WOMAN: That son of a bitch was Jeremy Shapiro. Fifth grade.

BOOB 1: See, the problem is that their junk is hidden in their fruit of the looms. Nobody can measure their growth the way they can ours.

BOOB 2: If only their penises were on their faces. Long. Thin. Fat. Short. Stubby. Thick. Pretzel rod. Ramen noodle. Then, they'd understand.

WOMAN: Can't you guys push out just a little bit more? Take me to a B-cup?

BOOB 1: We can't.

WOMAN: You'd think I was asking for a D-cup.

BOOB 2: We had our genetic orders.

BOOB 1: We'd like to help.

BOOB 2: Accommodate.

BOOB 1: But we can't.

BOOB 2: We don't have it in us.

BOOB 1: Though the seemingly somewhat good news is that in the long run, gravity will get to us. It will make us longer.

WOMAN: What good will that do? I don't want to trip over you; I want to display you!

BOOB 2: Really Boob?

BOOB 1: Well it was something. I was just trying to offer her something.

BOOB 2: We're not supposed to talk about the *(whispers loudly)* gravitational pull. You know that.

WOMAN: You think your inevitable droop is a comfort to me?!

BOOB 1: I thought --- .

WOMAN: You didn't think!

BOOB 2: You didn't think.

BOOB 1: What choices do we have here? She is clearly unhappy with us.

WOMAN: It's not that I'm unhappy. It's just that *(a beat)* okay, so I'm unhappy.

BOOB 2: It's not like we didn't know.

BOOB 1: All those years.

BOOB 2: How'd it go? *(thinks, then)* I must, I must, I must --- increase my bust.

BOOB 1: Cheerleading for boobs.

WOMAN: It didn't work.

BOOB 2: It's not like we didn't want to be talked into it. I mean, a bigger us would have meant notoriety, awe, acclaim, oogling --- .

BOOB 1: We would have liked that very much.

BOOB 2: It's not like anybody ever says, 'ooh, look at her boobs; now there's a pair with personality.'

BOOB 1: Nobody much cares for a small pair with a big personality.

BOOB 2: You know --- come to think on it, there is a solution to all of this.

BOOB 1: Really? Whisper it to me. *(#2 whispers to #1)* The padded bra! Of course.

WOMAN: You two need a padded room in a mental hospital is what you need, not a padded bra.

BOOB 2: Padded bras are soft and comfortable and they present themselves well in sweaters and shirts.

WOMAN: No more padded bras, you hear? There was a guy who took me out to dinner once, and when it came right down to it, he was very unhappy when the bra came off. 'Where did they go?' he asked, looking around to see if maybe he had touched some 'deflate' button by mistake. I coyly explained the situation to him. The jerk wanted to sue me for misrepresentation of my breasts.

BOOB 1: You're so unhappy.

WOMAN: I'm so unhappy.

BOOB 2: Couldn't you be just a little unhappy, maybe, with some other body part for awhile? It would help take the pressure off of us up here.

BOOB 1: Excellent idea, Boob.

BOOB 2: Why thank you, Boob. It, like all of a sudden, just came to me. Out of the blue.

BOOB 1: Out of the boob.

BOOB 2: Let's see. Who could you be as equally disappointed with as us, more so even? Hmm.

BOOB 1: Hmm indeed.

BOOB 2: Aha! I've got it!

BOOB 1: Give it over here, sister-friend!

BOOB 2: Lady, you can be pissed off with your kidneys!

WOMAN: I don't even know my kidneys.

BOOB 1: I'll make the introductions: Kidney 1 and 2, meet the female; female,meet the Kidneys.

WOMAN: I don't feel anything.

BOOB 2: Well, there are others to hate on: like your liver. Gall bladder, maybe. How about the ovaries? Now that's an organ to hate on --- responsible for periods, cramping, bloating, emotional unrest and hostility. It's positively a revolution down there every month.

WOMAN: How do you girls feel about --- implants?

BOOB 1: Don't you know what that means to a breast?

BOOB 2: And to the other one?

BOOB 1: They would cut us.

BOOB 2: And stuff us.

WOMAN: Enough! Both of you.

BOOB 1: Well apparently we're not.

WOMAN: It's not that I don't like you girls, I do, and I appreciate what you have tried to do here. It's just that I feel like you're holding me back.

BOOB 2: It's a shame we can't just get up and go somewhere where we'd be appreciated.

WOMAN: I want balance. I want harmony. I want boobs that sing out for all to hear. Flat-chested is not exactly the fashion statement I want to make anymore.

BOOB 1: Shit. She almost has me convinced.

BOOB 2: You want harmony? You want balance? Take a yoga class. Eat some bran.

WOMAN: Can't you work with me here? Please.

BOOB 1: Compromise?

BOOB 2: I think I can.

BOOB 1: We're willing to compromise. *(a beat)* The push-up bra it is. Even though it smushes us and folds us into unnatural positions and contorts us, and quite frankly, gives us one helluva boob ache.

BOOB 2: There. Happy now?

WOMAN: Yeah, well, it's just not for the dress for the party tonight. I might, you know, want to go push-up on other days, too.

BOOB 1: Here we go. Give an inch --- .

BOOB 2: She takes a cup size.

WOMAN: Like to work. And to the grocery, and maybe the gym because you never know who you're going to meet, and --- .

THE END

The Jennifer Bourne Identity

by Hilary King

Produced by manhattan**theatre**source *in Program C of EstroGenius 2012 with the following cast and crew:*

Director: Kathryn McConnell

Jennifer Bourne: Annalisa Loeffler*

Rob Bourne: Jeff Johnson

Sound Designer: Earline Stephen

Lighting Designer: Daisy Long

Stage Manager: Earlene Stephen

*Member of Actors' Equity Association

CONTACT
hilary.king@gmail.com

CHARACTERS
JENNIFER BOURNE— Female, 30s or 40s, modern American multitasking super mom

ROB BOURNE— Male, 30s or 40s, modern American male. JENNIFER'S husband

Setting: A modern kitchen/tv area.

Time: The present

Synopsis: When JENNIFER BOURNE *starts to remember her previous identity — before she became a multi-tasking supermom, she must decide if she wants to return to her slacker past or embrace a more dangerous future. A fun riff on the Jason Bourne movies.*

At rise: A modern suburban kitchen area with adjacent couch and tv area.

JENNIFER BOURNE, *a mother in her mid – to-late thirties, enters the kitchen. She takes a minute to take everything in. She sees everything. She misses nothing. When she moves, she walks quickly, confidently. She uses all her skills to make life work. On the way to the cooking area, using a hand or foot, she corrects the tipped chair, the open cabinet.*

She makes coffee, begins breakfast, doing all with great efficiency.

She crosses to the living room area to retrieve her laptop. As she passes the couch, she stops by it. A look of confusion crosses her face. Offstage, a toilet flushes. Startled, she resumes her work.

ROB *enters, half-asleep. As they pass, they kiss. She hands him a mug of coffee.*

ROB: Morning.

JENNIFER BOURNE: Morning.

ROB drinks coffee wakes up while JENNIFER continues her work.

JENNIFER: So: His soccer is at 10, on field 2. Her soccer is at 11, on field 5. Cleats are in the garage, uniforms are on their dressers. Oh, and we need to drop off the vacuum first. Ok?

JENNIFER *exits*

ROB: *(bleary-eyed)* Sure.

JENNIFER *returns holding a jumble of wrapping paper and loose ribbon.*

JENNIFER: He's got a birthday party at noon. After his game finishes, you meet me at her game. I'll take him and drop him off, hit the grocery store, then meet you at lunch. Got it?

JENNIFER *EXITS*

ROB: Not even close.

JENNIFER *reenters holding a perfectly wrapped gift with an elaborate bow.*

ROB: Wow. Impressive. Is that the Nerf thing in there?

JENNIFER: No, it's a politically-correct board game in which no one wins or loses or has fun. Honey--

She holds up the package.

JENNIFER: How do I know how to do this?

ROB: Beats me. I thought you took a class or something.

JENNIFER: I didn't take a class. I don't remember ever learning. How long have I been able to do it?

ROB: I don't know. Whenever we needed it done, you've been able to do it.

JENNIFER: Can you do it?

ROB: Why would I want to?

JENNIFER: What about this?

JENNIFER makes and plates breakfast using one hand and a knee.

ROB: Since we've had kids. You'd do that while holding a baby. Sometimes while holding two babies and making a conference call.

JENNIFER: Tell me: when you look around here what do you see?

JENNIFER gestures around the room.

ROB looks.

ROB: Bacon.

ROB moves toward bacon, eats some.

JENNIFER: Why don't I see that?

ROB: What do you see?

JENNIFER: The oven needs cleaning, we're out of paper towels, that door needs tightening, I need to pay the water bill, we haven't booked our the cabin for fall break, you should work on your relationship with your brother, we're not pushing the kids hard enough on their manners and I need to get my roots done. How come you don't see those things?

ROB; I see the important things. I see bacon. Jen, what's going on? Are you ok?

JENNIFER *crosses to the couch.*

ROB: What's wrong?

JENNIFER: Sometimes I get these images in my head. Pictures. Of a couch like this.

ROB: Well, yeah. You've had this couch forever. Since college.

JENNIFER: In these images, I'm lying on the couch. I think I'm watching tv. But I'm not doing anything! I'm not folding laundry. I'm not checking in at work. I'm not paying bills. I'm just—lying on the couch, watching tv. Is that possible?

ROB: You do that.

JENNIFER: When?

ROB: Last year, when you were sick, for an hour.

JENNIFER: But I have this image of me doing this for hours. Hours! Whole days of doing nothing! Was that me? Who was it? Who was I back then?

ROB: Sweetie, that was you, before you were married, before we had kids—

JENNIFER: Before I made partner? When people called me "Yes, ma'm" instead of "Mommy Mommy Mommy"?

ROB: Before you had it all and had to get it all done. You used to lie on this couch, in your pink sweat pants, hungover as hell, watching tv all weekend. Saturday, Sunday...

JENNIFER: *(horrified)* All weekend?

ROB: All weekend. Thursdays or Mondays too sometimes. Just watching tv. Chick flick after chick flick, Tory Spelling movie after Tory Spelling movie. You'd barely get up to go to the bathroom.

JENNIFER: That's disgusting!

ROB: You would even eat on the couch. Chips, ice cream, cookie dough. The pre-made kind, so you didn't have to, you know, actually make it. I don't think it was even organic.

JENNIFER: My God. All that free time. I just wasted it. I was horrible. I was a monster.

ROB: You were young. You were adorable. And totally hot. We had some good times right here. Lots of good times. Do you still have those pink sweatpants?

JENNIFER shakes her head.

ROB: Come here, sit down.

ROB leads JENNIFER to the couch. She reaches for laundry, laptop, etc.

ROB: Nope. Just sit.

JENNIFER: No laundry, no laptop?

ROB: *(pointing remote at tv)* Nope. So: tv on. Flipping channels. Let's see. Action movie about a spy with amnesia — oh, look, a chick flick. There's a girl, she's single, she's got a spunky best friend, they're gonna talk about shoes and boys---

Beat.

JENNIFER gets up and in a quick, Jason-Bourne type of move, pulls out knitting.

JENNIFER: While knitting baby booties for war orphans in Afghanistan?

In an equally Bourne-like move, ROB disarms her and with the remote pointed at her back like a gun, marches her back to the couch.

ROB: You used to be able to relax. You used to not care, at least not so much. I'm going to reprogram you so when you see this couch, you see a place to sit, not a place to sit while doing some chore that can be done while sitting. So, sit. Stare.

JENNIFER: Yes, let's do that! I want to see that. I want to see a couch. And bacon. And nothing else. Reprogram me. Reprogram me to relax. I would love to relax. I want to relax. Let's do it.

ROB: You're doing it now.

JENNIFER: I am?

ROB: You would be if you would stop talking and become completely absorbed in this fascinating program on fish--

ROB zones out. JENNIFER looks at him then at the tv.

JENNIFER: I wish I could do that. Why can't I do that?

JENNIFER stands up.

JENNIFER: Who did this to me? Who put this in my head — this non-stop monologue of all things I need to do, and all things I need to be? Mom, wife, career woman, skinny, sexy, polite, kind, giving, ambitious, industrious, ambidextrous —

JENNIFER sits down with a thud.

ROB: Honey, is there more bacon?

JENNIFER: Let me see--

JENNIFER starts to get up, then sits back down.

JENNIFER: I don't know. And if there is any, get it yourself.

ROB shrugs and continues watching tv.

JENNIFER: The world can starve and wear dirty socks. I'm just going to sit and stare.

ROB: See, it's relaxing.

Several beats pass. JENNIFER tries to relax, fails, tries. Then she stops trying.

ROB: You're recharging your batteries. You're chilling out.

JENNIFER: You're right, honey. I should do this more often.

JENNIFER leans into her ROB'S arms on the couch. When he wraps his arms around her, she takes the remote from him, Bourne-like.

ROB: What are you doing? You're supposed to —
JENNIFER points the remote at the tv.

JENNIFER: Sports Center.

ROB *immediately zones out.*

JENNIFER *stands up, still near the couch.*

JENNIFER: I can't do it. I was a different person then. I don't want to relax. I don't want to be reprogrammed. You know what recharges my batteries now? Getting stuff done. I've got a house to run, a family to manage, a job to do. And there are dreams I haven't even dreamed yet. Ambitions I don't even know I have yet. I want to embrace that, not the cookie-dough eating slacker I was in my twenties. I may be tired, cranky and forever in a ponytail but the world is my oyster and I want pearl earrings. Even if I have to go out and catch the oyster and make the damn earrings myself. So, no. No sit-and-stare for me. I'm going to kick butt and enjoy it.

JENNIFER *starts to move away from couch.*

ROB *grabs her arm.*

ROB: *(whispering)* Don't do it. They'll write articles about you. The New York Times. Time, Newsweek. They'll write long, whiny articles that will get referred back to other long, whiny articles. Then they'll put you on the Today Show.

JENNIFER: Why?

ROB: *(whispering)* They can't sell you things if you're happy...

Beat

JENNIFER: How about some more bacon, hon?

ROB: Yes, please.

JENNIFER *goes and gets bacon for her* ROB, *brings it to him with a kiss. She returns to the kitchen, humming happily. She makes breakfast, perfects the birthday bow.*

JENNIFER: *(to herself as she fixes the bow)* Yeah, that's good. You know, I think I wanna do a triathlon this year. Maybe start my own business. Jewelry. No—oil. Yeah, oil. That's where the power is.

ROB: I really need to get up off the couch and catch up with you, don't I?

ROB gets up and tries his hand at multitasking. He almost fails. JENNIFER reaches to help him, but he manages it alone, barely.

JENNIFER: You'll catch up someday. You'll have to. For now, just leave the birthday parties and car chases to me. God, I love a good car chase. You get so many errands done on the way.

JENNIFER resumes her work.

ROB: *(pointing remote at tv)* Honey, look, Tori Spelling!

JENNIFER whips around, pulls out a gun and fires at the tv.

JENNIFER: I can't stand Tori Spelling.

THE END

Rosie the Retired Rockette©

by Daniel Guyton

Produced by manhattan**theatre**source *in Program C of EstroGenius 2012 with the following cast and crew:*

Director: Heather Cohn

Rosie: Vivian Meisner*

Dawn: Kristen Vaughan

Christie: Marianne Miller*

Ella: Monica Furman

Sound Designer: Earline Stephen

Lighting Designer: Daisy Long

Stage Manager: Earlene Stephen

*Member of Actors" Equity Association

CONTACT
dguyton21@gmail.com

© The script cannot be included due to copyright issues.

With Sola Voce, EstroGenius provides solo artists the opportunity to bring their distinctive visions to the stage.

Sailing Down the Amazon

Written by Rosanna Yamigiwa Alfaro; performed by June Lewin* and directed by Victoria Marsh

alfaros@comcast.net

Tea With Vivien Leigh

Written and performed by Alessandre Drapos

alessandradrapos@gmail.com

Happily Never After

Written & performed by Gina Femia

ginafemia@gmail.com

Cheap Chicken

Written & performed by Maria Gabriele*; directed by Deborah Hedwall

mariagabriele2000@yahoo.com

Out of My Mind

Written & performed by Laura Pruden*

laurapruden@gmail.com

Octopus

Written & performed by Stephanie Shaw

shawsall@sbcglobal.net

If You're Feeling Blue, Paint Yourself a Different Color !

Written & performed by Stephanie Shaw

shawsall@sbcglobal.net

Sailing Down the Amazon

The deafening sound of parrots and howler monkeys. A boat sailing down the Amazon. Three deck chairs and a small table with a pitcher of lemonade and two glasses. RIMA, 80 is sitting in the middle chair. We imagine her sleeping husband, Sam on one side, a young woman on the other. She holds a large bouquet of pink roses and speaks to the young woman. RIMA repeats herself a good deal, but each repetition should be said fresh, as if for the first time.

Beautiful, aren't they? Take a sniff. They have a lovely pink aroma. Let's tell Sam when he wakes up that the whole boat pitched in and bought them for him. Otherwise he'll toss them overboard. *(beat)* They're actually for me from Marcus. I don't know how he found me here in the middle of the jungle. Well, he's an actor. Dramatic gestures come easily to him. Sam says he can't be trusted. He says, "Marcus manufactures the impulse"... "Marcus bonds with Velcro." But, then, I've known the man for fifty years. After our first show together he sent me a lovely bouquet of roses, and before they wilted, another arrived at the door. Sam took a dim view of the proceedings. *(She laughs loudly.)*

No. No. Don't worry. Nothing wakes him, not even the screeching parrots. He always sleeps like a log. And today. Well, after all the excitement, he probably won't get up until it's time to go to bed. Not that I'm complaining. I put my finger under his nose every two minutes to make sure he's still breathing. What a scare.

(She smells the roses.) Marcus always wants to get together on Christmas and New Year's Eve. On Valentine's Day too, he's so outrageous. *(She rummages through her purse.)* You can't change a leopard's spots. Especially if he's an old leopard. Every few weeks he sends me a long letter en Francais. I have one in here. *(She pulls out the letter.)* You don't know French? *Quel dommage.* Then you can't read it. Neither can Sam. Sam is impervious to foreign languages.

I keep thinking I have to write a postcard. Then I realize it's a postcard to my mother, my dead mother whom I loved more than anyone else in the world. What? *(She adjusts her hearing aid which lets out a piercing sound.)* Oh dear. *(She readjusts it so the sound stops.)* I'm sorry. He - this one here - *(She affectionately pokes Sam)* usually

acts as my ears. Do you know French? *(beat) Quel dommage.* Then
you can't read it. *(She stuffs the letter back in her purse.)* Sam can't
either. He's impervious to foreign languages.

What are you doing, spending New Year's Eve talking to an old
woman on a boat in the middle of the jungle? I've always thought
there was something sad, something wrong with young people who
hang out with their elders. *(beat)* What were we talking about? *(She
looks down at the bouquet.)* Oh yes, we were talking about Marcus.
My hand was resting on the subject. It's an old actor's trick. Pick
up the prop, and it sets off the line.
Well, Sam says Marcus has become old and stupid. Not at all like
the rest of us, of course. Also he says Marcus smells bad, the
opposite of his roses. He says even when Marcus is on the other
side of the room there's a little bit of him in the air and in your
nostrils. Still, the man wants to run off with an 80-year-old woman.
(She hugs the roses.) That's quite something, isn't it?
Just now when you tilted your head that way you looked very
beautiful. No really. The way your hair fell. I used to have hair
like that. What? *(beat)* You're right. *(She pats her hair.)* It's still
looking fine, isn't it? I have a lovely hairdresser in New York who's
Japanese. His name's Luigi.
(She takes a drink of lemonade.) Oh, dear. It's so hot, and this
lukewarm lemonade's not making things any better. That catfish
they gave us for lunch is still flopping about inside my stomach.
(She swats herself of the leg.) I've also been bitten by every insect in
the jungle. Fortunately at 80 everything travels more slowly
through the system - it'll be a month or two before I know whether
I've caught something dreadful on this cruise - malaria, maybe, or
something worse – those pink bird droppings are everywhere. This
problem *(She points to her ear)* I got from my mother. She gave me
her beauty, but she also gave me her deafness. She said, "When
you're old and deaf, Rima, always enter the room talking. Don't
stop to catch your breath. Don't allow anyone else to speak."

Forgive me. You become an egomaniac when you get old. You talk
about your ears that are deaf, your swollen legs, your irregular
heartbeat. "De hand, d'arma, de bilbow... de nick, et de sin." *(As*

she speaks she shows off each of her parts quite fetchingly.) You don't
have a clue what I'm talking about, do you? Never mind.
(She greets a fellow passenger) Hello! Hello! Yes, we're doing fine,
thank you. He's happily napping as you see. He's been asleep all
afternoon so he'll be a nuisance all night. *(She speaks to the young
woman after the person passes.)* Who was that? *(beat)* People have to
be very interesting these days, or they go straight into the
irretrievable file. If I don't like what they're saying, I switch this off.
(She indicates her hearing aid.)
Life is very sad. Just when you reach the age where you get it all
together, your mind begins to go. Your brain is no longer connected
to your mouth. I've been having these glitches. Terrifying little
glitches. *(She checks Sam's breathing.)* You think he has his
problems, but they're nothing compared to mine. No. Don't laugh.
I was at the doctor's two weeks ago because I was worried about
my memory. And he gave me all these tests. Count backwards
from 100 by 7's. *(beat)* That's right. Who can do that at any age?
Fortunately I'd been warned about that one. You subtract 10 and
add 3. I think I did that rather well. Then he said, list the
Presidents backwards. Why do they ask you to do everything
backwards? Because they know you're having difficulty moving
forward? Because it's their job to put obstacles in your way?
The doctor got a call from his wife and sent me back out to the
crowded waiting room. A half hour later he emerged and said to
me in front of all these people - very loudly, so I could hear him -
"Well, it looks to me like Alzheimer's." Just like that, the pigfucker.
(She laughs.) It was like being given the death sentence. *(beat)* I
know. Horrible. It was horrible of him. I was supposed to
schedule an MRI, but I booked a cruise instead. That's why we're
here - sailing down the Amazon.

I told Sam I wanted to get as far away from home as possible for
New Year's. Sam said, as he always says, "Your command is my
wish." I said I'd rather be here with the famous blue cannibals than
with my friends in Manhattan. I haven't told any of them about
this. Thank God, Sam couldn't have children. I wouldn't want them
to see me in this state.

There's no cure for Alzheimer's, you know. They can slow it down, but they can't stop it. They'll probably put me on Aricept - a friend of mine is using it. She hasn't noticed any change in her memory, but it's affected her bladder. She has to wear a harness that hitches up here. *(She lifts up her skirt.)* Oh, you're right. Someone might pass by.

I've become like those frantic people you see on the TV news, piling sandbags on the banks of a swollen river. No matter what they do they can't stop it. They can slow it down, but they can't stop it. I find life doesn't straighten itself out. Instead it coils around and ends up strangling you. *(beat)* What? *(beat)* No, you don't understand. I'm sorry, but you can't possibly begin to understand what I'm feeling. *(Tears come to her eyes.)*

(She stands up.) I worry I'll forget everything that ever happened to me, but the brain's a funny thing. They say people who have no memory at all can still ride a bike or play the piano. There has to be a difference between the kind of memory that deals - or doesn't deal - with facts and numbers and the kind connected to the emotions. Well, I'm convinced those memories go to a different part of the brain. You never forget those. For instance, something that Marcus said to me fifty years ago or the sensation when he first put his hand on - well, never mind. I still remember everything.

Marcus and I - we were in so many plays together. People think anyone can act, that it's as natural as walking and talking. But the fact is it's the most difficult thing in the world, and Marcus and I were very good at it - shows in New York, then tours across the country. This one *(She indicates Sam.)* insisted on coming along. He said we shouldn't be apart because "tragic things" could happen when you're apart. That's what he said, "tragic things." And, of course, he was right. Tragic things do happen when you're apart. *(beat)* And when you're together as well.

Marcus and I were cast together so often we knew how to dance together verbally, how to tango, how to waltz. How to follow, to dip. If it's done well, you can lose yourself in mutual adoration, and everyone on the dance floor will notice, the spotlight will find you. I remember a review in the New York Times – I bet I have it perfectly. It said, "These two first-class actors have been paired so often that they hardly have to act to seem like a comfortably married couple." It's hard for me to describe my feelings towards Marcus. He's like a brother to me, but we have this slightly incestuous relationship.

I remember riding with him on a crowded subway after one of our first shows. I must have been about your age. We were sitting pressed together because there were these two very fat people on either side of us. And I imagined that we were in bed. The feeling was heightened because Marcus actually fell asleep, he was so exhausted after a matinee and evening performance. It was a long five minutes between stops, being an express train. I deliberately slowed down my breathing to match his. He lurched forward when the train stopped, and I caught hold of him in my arms.

Sam, of course, hates Marcus. *(She checks his breathing.)* But he puts up with him. You could say I expect too much of life and Sam expects too little. He goes to church to learn humility. I go to the theater for ecstasy. You don't get much of that at the Episcopal Church. Sam never flirted like Marcus. He just fell in love. This man has devoted his entire life to me.

Marcus might not be as devoted as Sam, but he has this incredible warmth. You get close to him and you're wrapped up in this cocoon of warmth. He's like a brother to me, but we have this slightly incestuous relationship. I remember once we were sitting together in a subway – pressed on both sides by two very fat people – and he fell asleep. I closed my eyes and pretended we were in bed together. When the train stopped he lurched forward, and I caught him in my arms.

(She answers the greeting of another passenger.) Hello, Nat! Yes, we're doing fine, thank you. *(She checks his breathing.)* Still alive. *(beat)* Right. Drinks at 7. *(beat)* No, I hadn't forgotten, but you're right to remind me. I have to be brought up to date every ten minutes. *(She waves good-bye to him.)* The one New Yorker on this boat – Nat Gardner, the playwright, a horrible man. *(beat)* You know how some men notice your hands, your hair, or your voice? Well, Nat notices your Achilles heel and goes after it. He's an Achilles heel person. He stares at me across the table at dinner exactly the way we stared at those poor villagers we visited on shore yesterday - those pathetic

descendants of the famous blue cannibals.

Last night, thanks to Nat, I saw white flashes in the corner of my right eye. He had his short wave radio on – the pigfucker has the cabin next to ours - and it was on so loud you couldn't hear the music, only the throbbing. Well, I listened to this for ten minutes, and it literally drove me insane. I banged on the walls. I started shouting. Obscenities - that's what Sam tells me - vile, inappropriate thoughts you should only say on stage. Sam had to hold me back from going out to the corridor and kicking down his door. That's scary, isn't it? I've become a monster.
Maybe that's what made Sam do what he did - I mean, pretty soon I might fly off the handle at the slightest provocation. That happens, doesn't it, to people in my condition. They become violent. They have to be calmed down and drugged up. When I banged on the walls and acted like a madwoman, Sam must have been frightened to death. That's the real reason, I think, that he jumped overboard last night. Escaping from all this. He was so desperate about my condition it sent him right over the railing.

Oh, I know he said he tripped and fell. When they fished him out of the water he was genuinely embarrassed. He blamed himself for being such a klutz, and it's true, he's such a klutz. He's a stumbler – he'd trip over a blade of grass. But to climb over a railing and jump into the river? Let's not kid ourselves. It was a deliberate, profoundly hostile act. He wanted to drown himself and leave me high and dry. When I saw him splashing about in the water I wondered where the crocodiles and piranhas were, not to mention the blue cannibals. They all seem to have been caught napping.
I had a dream last night - after I finally got to sleep. I dreamt I had awakened from a dream and found my mother lying in bed with me and Sam. She took my hand and held it. Very tenderly. It was a very nice experience. *(She checks his breathing.)* Still breathing. He's probably dreaming he's dead. Look at that smile on his face. He's thinking how nice and peaceful it is far away from me in his watery grave. *(beat)* After a certain point everything comes unglued at the seams. Have you noticed how many people die in December? *(She checks Sam's breathing.)* It's difficult to cross from

one year to another. Luckily it looks like Sam's going to make it to the other side. Luckily they fished him out of the river.

Before we left New York I forced Sam to buy me some pills to put in the bank deposit vault - just in case things got too unbearable. Now the first thing I have to remember to do when I get back is to take those pills out of the vault. I have to make sure Sam doesn't get there before I do.

(She picks up the roses and goes to the ship's railing.) It's getting dark. I should throw these flowers overboard before he wakes up, a nice treat for the crocodiles. *(She is interrupted by several explosions and flashes of light.)* What was that? It sounded like an explosion or gunshots. *(She shouts.)* Can someone tell me what's happening to us? Are the fucking blue cannibals attacking us? *(to young woman)* No! No! I'm fine! I don't want to sit down! Get your hands off me! And don't look at me like that, you condescending little twit. *(She pulls herself together.)* I see my poor husband's finally awake. Could you please leave us? I'd like to be alone with him.
(She crouches by Sam's chair.) Don't worry, darling. We're perfectly safe. I'm right here beside you. *(More explosions and flashes.)* Stop shaking, dear. Stop it at once. It's nothing, nothing. It's only the villagers with their firecrackers. *(beat)* What about the roses? *(She turns away from him.)* I really can't hear you.
Isn't this amazing? There was no one, and now there're hundreds on the shore. *(Singing and chanting.)* Look over there. It's a torch light procession. How beautiful! Oh, they're wading into the water. *(beat)* No, darling, I don't think they're intending to swim all the way to the boat. Look at the women throwing flowers into the water. An offering to the river god. Well, I have flowers too, don't I? There! *(She ceremoniously tosses the roses overboard as the sky becomes dazzlingly bright.)* Happy New Year, Marcus! God bless!

THE END

Tea With Vivien Leigh

AN INTRODUCTION:

"It takes a certain type of woman to play Blanche Dubois and Scarlett O'Hara," said the English man as he stereotypically sipped his tea. I nodded, not really knowing what he meant. He looked up as if he had just discovered what *he* really meant himself. Sternly, he declared,
"You've got to have a **crack**."

This was the first day I learned about actress Vivien Leigh with my director, Philip Hedley. Previous to this day, before my research, I only knew Vivien Leigh as that *unfairly* gorgeous woman in "Gone with the Wind." Shortly after my initial desire to research the actress, I soon learned what my director meant by the "crack."

Today, we would classify Vivien Leigh as having "manic depression," or "bi-polar disorder," sprinkled with a bit of nymphomania. The parallel between the two infamous roles Vivien played were uncannily and eerily familiar to her personal life at the time she played them. Vivien Leigh battled with mental imprisonment, a dysfunctional, everlasting, love with Laurence Olivier, alcoholism, fame, image, and nymphomania. Many of her friends and colleagues recall her spewing out the lines of Scarlett O' Hara and Blanche DuBois in her *own* life during the rehearsal process, and even years after having been away from the set.

I wanted to make this play accessible to everyone, not just experts on Vivien Leigh or older English thespians. Vivien Leigh dominates the setting of this play in a master-class situation gone horrendously wrong. At the time of the play, Vivien is retiring at her home in the English countryside post mental breakdown.

In 1952 while filming William Dieterle's "Elephant Walk," Vivien had to be escorted off set and back to England due to extremely outlandish behavior, such as running around naked on the set for an example. Laurence Olivier had to fly to Ceylon against her will in order to assure she recuperated. Because of this fiasco, her spirits are low (to say at the least.)

What better person to make Vivien feel fabulous again than a young naïve American drama student/aspiring actress? After a short amount of time spent away from the set of "Elephant Walk," Vivien Leigh was replaced by actress Elizabeth Taylor. Originally, actor Peter Finch broke the news to Vivien Leigh in person. He recalls Vivien "with eyes of fury," screaming the famous lines of Blanche DuBois, "Get out of here quick before I start screaming fire!"

In the case of the play, Vivien receives a phone call from Peter Finch, and the young girl gets the wrath at the end of the meeting, which was supposed to be a delightful session of passing wisdom and sipping tea. (There is a chair where the girl would be sitting, however, physically there is no one actually sitting there. By the end of the play, whether or not you think there was ever someone there in the first place is up to you.)

Vivien Leigh transforms from the perfect ladylike hostess she was known to be, to the out of control excessively passionate woman she couldn't *help* but be. Gradually, the audience witnesses a breakdown. Vivien snaps back and forth from the "Perfect Vivien Leigh", to Scarlett O'Hara, to Blanche DuBois. Most of the lines spoken by Vivien in this script are taken from actual letters she wrote, or written anecdotes passed down by credible sources such as Laurence Olivier, actor Alan Dent, Noel Coward, actress Claire Bloom, and the lover she died with, Jack Merivale.

One could argue this: in order to be talented, you must be aware of the presence of reality versus the make believe. One could also argue that it is an actor's *job* to become engulfed. If this is so, Ms. Leigh exceeds all expectations. Winner of two academy awards, Vivien Leigh puts more than blood, sweat, and tears into each project. In a teatime setting, we quickly learn that theatre and life are fiercely united. Vivien's roles are her escape from mental illness…but are they ultimately her demise?

Lights Up. Vivien sits in her elegant living room playing solitaire.
There is a knock at the door.

VIVIEN: Just a second!
  (Beat.) A moment. *(She begins to dance.)*

Yes, yes come in! They're playing our tune my dear!
So nice to meet you. Your name?

(Her dance breaks as the music fades.)
Your name, dear?
(Beat.)
What a lovely name.
  (Beat.)
Well, do sit down ...I'm not the queen you mustn't wait for an invitation.
I want every guest here at Notley Abbey to be comfortable, as if they were at home. Do you take sugar and milk in your tea?
(Beat.)
(She brings tea from the bar to the table and pours.)

I understand you're about to play Blanche DuBois at your drama centre.
(Beat.)
Oh, now don't say that darling I'm sure you'll be absolutely lovely.
I take it you've seen my film...yes.
I was just working on a new film last week, actually. Peter Finch and I are starring in Elephant Walk together. I felt-tired, so,
...luckily for you, I...took a short holiday to return here to England.
(Beat.)
You may have read that I've not been well...but I was simply exhausted from the filming! And it is terribly hot in Ceylon!
(Beat.)
Larry flew me back to England. He has been away often, I am sorry he isn't here today. If he were, he'd be out pruning trees! That's his hobby.
Care for a cigarette?
(Beat.)

A lot of things are bad for you, dear…do try to have a bit of fun or life won't be very exciting now, will it?
(Beat. A fiery grin stretches her lips as she lights the girl's cigarette.)
Good girl.
(Pause. She lights her own.)
Yes, dear. Not at all, darling.
(Beat.)
Actors ask that question often: "How did you get started?"

Well, dear, I suppose if I were to give you any advice, I'd tell you… acting is life. That is what it should be. I don't know what the "Method" is.
When I was sent away from India to Catholic school in England, the first day I arrived, the mother superior asked, "What would you like to be when you grow up Vivi?" And I said, "I am going to be a great actress."
(Beat.)
I attended the Royal Academy of Dramatic Art. I'm sure I must have learned something….but ask anyone and they will tell you it was a complete waste of time.
(Beat.)
I do enjoy film, but the stage is where my heart lies. It's the only place I feel…dangerous and safe. You see, danger is my safety. The stage is a great challenge. And it takes great discipline. But when I come into the theatre at night, I get that sense of security…I get in early; an hour and a half before curtain up. And I say the part over to myself every night, however well I know it-not aloud, just to myself…..
 And I practice it just the way Larry and I rehearse it the night before. His notes always make such a difference.
(Beat.)
I am rather lucky…I have a splendid career.
(Beat.)
Yes…"Gone with the Wind."
I suppose that's why I'm here! Everyone asks me about the same things; "Gone with the Wind," Laurence Olivier, and "Streetcar named Desire."
(She gives the girl a bewitching smile and crushes the cigarette into the ash

tray.)

"Gone With the Wind!"

I suppose it all started when I made a complete ass of myself attempting to ski in Kitzbühel. I broke my ankle, and was forced to remain in the cabin for a week, so I ended up buying Margarett Mitchell's "Gone with The Wind." From the moment I read it, I was fascinated by the lovely, wayward, tempestuous Scarlett. And when I heard that the book was to be filmed in Hollywood early 1939 I longed to play the part.

I have always believed that if you want something with all your heart and soul you get it. "I am going to play Scarlett," I said to myself-time and time again, "I am going to play Scarlett."

Larry said I pursued the role with "an almost demonic determination."

Well, I must have read the book over a hundred times. Eventually, I was to bring it with me on set. By the end of filming, nearly every page was dog-eared.

The search for Scarlett had taken two years, it cost $92,000 and included 1,400 candidates…of whom ninety had screen tests.

And little 'ol me….a 'nobody' from England: without an American agent stole the role!

So, you see darling, I did have to attack the role as if I were the devil. And in this case, the devil won.

(Beat.)

But, let me tell you, it was a bloody long time coming.

I remember sending in photo after photo of myself dressed as Scarlett! Oh, and then Larry came storming in during one of my sessions to tell me that Ava Gardner had been announced in the papers as Scarlett O'Hara.

Well, I knew it couldn't have been true. They hadn't met me yet.

I was actually given a role in a promising American film that everyone urged me to accept. But it interfered with the filming of "Gone with the Wind," so I told them I wasn't interested.

I was even due to start rehearsals for a production at the Old Vic. I knew it wasn't going to happen. I was going to America. I told my agent not to worry… "I'd only be gone for a few days."

I didn't see England for nearly a year after that.
On my way across the Atlantic I read and re-read "Gone With the Wind." I did not sleep. Of course, I've never slept much, ever. Since I was born, I've never slept much!

I knew I would detest Hollywood but I didn't know how much. I had no intention of being there for too long because it would be difficult to take stage engagements between films. And I vowed not to neglect the theatre, whatever happened. I'd rather be a Misses Patrick Campbell than a Greta Garbo.

I..I went to California. I met Larry at the Beverly Hills hotel, and then, a few hours later, after our marvelous reunion, he introduced me to Myron Selznick...The brother of the producer of "Gone with the Wind."

Larry took me by the hand, walked me right into the hotel lounge and introduced me as "someone who might possibly be of extraordinary interest."
I offered Myron my hand, as he took it he looked me up and down...and then Larry quickly interjected, saying that he ought to take me down to meet David Selznick on the set. David...the producer of the film. Understand?

The next day, absolutely terrified...I came into the studio wearing that gorgeous full-length mink Larry gave me for Christmas, a dark halo hat set back just enough so that my face could be seen. My hair fell shoulder length, and my make-up was applied by a professional who had been told to "use his imagination," and do a "Scarlett O'Hara face."
(Beat.)
Oh!....I looked lovely.
I was then instructed to meet David Selznick on the set while they were filming the epic burning of Atlanta scene.
"Cut!" was called.
It was dead silent.
Across the set Myron shouted to his brother:
"Hey genius, meet your Scarlett O'Hara."

A few moments after meeting David, he invited me to read with
George Cukor...whom we understood was to be the director.
Cukor was pleased with my reading. He told Selznick that I ought
to have an official screen test scheduled for the following week.
Until then, I worked with Cukor on my interpretation. He was
magnificent. He understood art. I was mesmerized by his
magnetism; he was constantly flowing with an almost palpably
charged energy. He started calling me Scarlett the first day I met
him!
(A slight pause.)
I suppose while Scarlett wasn't the most easy-going type, neither
am I. I cannot let well enough alone. I get restless...
(Beat.)
The day of the screen test I rushed to the set hours early. I had been
up all night in anticipation. I waited outside the costume
department until the dresser returned from lunch. Then I slipped
into that crinoline dress...still warm.
There could hardly have been time for the previous actress to get
out of it.
As if that weren't enough, they didn't even have Leslie Howard to
do the test with me.
But I "rose above it!" And my audition, including the Southern
accent which came so easily to me...impressed them.
The next day, in George Cukor's backyard... by the pool... David
handed me the contract and said "I guess we're stuck with you."
(Beat.)
Oh! Mind you, if you'd seen the takes of the poor American girls
before me; shaking their ringlets and swishing their crinolines
without a thought in their pretty little heads, crying, "Oh Ashley
you do love me!"... you would have known the choice was
inevitable.
(Beat.)
....Yes, I'm sure to you, this all must sound...simply marvelous.
Looking back it's considerably difficult to remember any elation
towards the process because filming the thing was a bloody pain in
the ass.

It took nine months. Every day. Nine AM sharp with elocution lessons for the accent, then wardrobe fittings. I had thirty one changes of costume...

And it all went further and further downhill after they sacked dear George and replaced him with the chauvinistic prick, known as "Victor Fucking Fleming."

You see, I've never thought men were all that important...and Victor considered himself a "man's man" because, before he became a director *(and a massive wanker)* he was an air force pilot!

Every morning he'd say "I'm giving up this industry to return to shooting tigers!" And every morning I'd mutter, "End my misery and bloody do so."

You know that line Scarlett always bellowed, "fiddle-dee-dee?" Yes, well, Victor decided that was to be my name.

"Fiddle-dee-dee, don't hold your face that way the angle makes you look awful."

...He called me a "strange beauty."

(Mockingly.)"Fiddle-dee-dee, stick to the revised script!"

... The bloody idiot hadn't even read the actual script before taking the bloody job.

Ah, yes..."Why don't you take your script and stick it up your Royal British Ass?!" is what he said to me.

And I'll never forget the humiliating day he expressed his dissatisfaction with my breasts in front of the entire crew:

"For Christ's sake, they're too small...tape em up! Let's get a good look at Fiddle-dee-dee's TITS!"

(Beat.)

I blame it all on Gable. If it weren't for that lazy, incoherent epitome of a "screen personality", George never would have been sacked. Gable thought George was a "woman's director." He was jealous of the time he was spending on Scarlett, nervous that his direction would cause me to overshadow his role. As if his role stood a chance in the first place. Luckily I, secretly, rehearsed with Cukor throughout the production.

We'd work all night. I never wanted to stop! Well, I didn't have to when Larry came to visit because he insisted we rehearse the scenes as he played "Ashley" and, ha! "Mammy." I looked forward to those nights.

 I was so lonely during the day. I couldn't help but think about Leigh *(my first husband)*…and the baby.

(Beat.)

Gable continued to lack any sense of creativity and energy. I'll never understand how he could leave the set so promptly at 6p.m. as though he held an office job. I was so fed up one night I screamed, "What are you fucking about for?" All my effort was to no avail. Ignorance was tolerated, and Gable was allowed to do as he pleased.

(Beat.)

That kind of behavior would never stand in the theatre. I suppose that's why Clark was never invited to the stage. Oh…that, and the fact his breath was so awful, the stench could probably be smelt from upstage all the way to the very last row of the gallery.

(Beat.)

I'll never forget the day I met him. I had been late for a rehearsal due to a …scheduling issue. And when I arrived, I heard Gable scream, "With a dame like that; I think I'll walk out of this picture!" Then from behind him, I said: "I quite agree, Mr. Gable. If I were a man, I'd tell that Vivien Leigh to go straight back to England and fuck herself!"

He laughed of course, and forgave me. He said "Damn it, you're right!" and we embraced.

(Beat.)

Some people called me manic.

But it wasn't that. I was…determined.

I didn't mind that the shooting took all night because I wanted it to be perfect.

And, the harder I worked the sooner it would be over and I could finally get back to Larry.

Oh! That last bloody scene before the interval was the death of me. I'm sure I have spoken the lines, "As God is my witness, I'll never be hungry again," more times than I've taken a piss. That scene was shot over and over again almost every day because the fucking sun failed to rise in the right fucking place at the right fucking time.

(In a fit of rage she flies from her seat and stomps in front of the girl to demonstrate.)
"ACTION"
(Vivien mimics the famous scene from "Gone with the Wind.")
"AS GOD IS MY WITNESS, I'LL NEVER BE HUNGRY AGAIN!"

"CUT!" "AGAIN!"

(Rapidly, she repeats the scene twice more.)

UGHHH! UP YOURS!

Oh! I refused to make the vomit noise, actually. It was far too ridiculous-very unladylike. Olivia De Havilland volunteered to dub it over for me.
What a doll, she was.
(Beat.)
It was Hollywood that was getting to me. I don't mean to insult you, dear, but I do not think there is anything nice about America...except for the football...and the politeness of men in garages. And I couldn't stand not seeing Larry. Thank God they "allowed" me to have a break where I could be with him!
He was doing a play in New York at the time, we met halfway at a hotel in Kansas City, we went upstairs, and we fucked and we fucked and we fucked the whole weekend!
Well, you need some joy out of life!
(A slight pause.)
Scarlett had one thing I hope I never have: Selfish egotism.
Scarlett was a fascinating person whatever she did, but she was never a good person. She was too petty, too self-centered...
(As Scarlett O'Hara.)
"No I won't think about that now...I'll think about that tomorrow."
(Beat.)
Well...Why don't we have a toast to the girl, shall we?
(She fills up a shot glass.)
TO SCARLETT!
(She finishes the drink in one swig and throws the glass against the wall.)
Oh, how silly of me! I've forgotten lunch. I have some delicious smoked salmon for you. Mmm I'm sure you'll enjoy every bite! I find American food to be quite tasteless!

(Pause.)
Good?
(Beat.)
I'm glad!
(Beat.)
How are you enjoying England?
(Beat.)
Have you a special gentleman companion in London?
(Beat.)
Oh, come now…you ought to have several! You are abroad.
(She gathers her cigarette case.)
Of course, do make sure they know what they're doing. It is quite common for a young girl to believe that "good looking" and "good in bed" are synonymous.
(Beat. She lights a cigarette.)
Yes, it is an attractive lighter isn't it? It's one of my many gifts from Larry.

Larry.

Larry.

Larry, Larry, Larry.
….I'm not sure who Larry worships more. Himself or….God.
(Beat.)
Yes, I met him long before I ventured into Hollywood. First time I ever laid eyes on him, he was playing Romeo. I had the opportunity to meet him backstage. I waited until he was alone. As he was taking off his make up …I snuck up behind him and planted a gentle kiss on the back of his neck.
He was mine. Just as it happened with my first husband; One look and I said, "I will marry him." Didn't matter whether he had a wife or not!
(Beat.)
I saw Larry in that play fourteen times. Soon, we were inseparable.
(Beat.)
I met his wife, Jill…eventually.

I decided to surprise them as a couple while they were vacationing in Capri! She took the liberty of inviting me to luncheon at their

several times. Silly woman…she told me everything about Larry.
Then she begged me not to appear with him in our first film
together! She knew their marriage was over. I suppose I'm going to
pay for what I've done.
(Beat.)
I am paying.
(Beat.)
We were "living in sin" until we both filed for divorce. I, from
Leigh, and he, from Jill. We both have a child from our previous
marriages.
I remember Larry rushing to the hospital where Jill was going into
labor- right after we had just made love! She probably smelt my
perfume during contractions…
Larry and I wanted a child of our own. During an intensely physical
scene on the set of Caesar and Cleopatra, I had to whip an African
slave and scurry up and down marble steps again and again. I was
fine the first day of filming, but then they ordered re-takes for
another day. I slipped going up the stairs, and well, I lost the baby.
It might have been worth it if I was filming a rendition of a
Shakespearian piece…but Shaw's "Newt of the Nile," was certainly
not deserving of a miscarriage!
(Beat.)
Well, it's quite alright! I "rose above it!" And besides, maternity is
such a messy business; I never want to do it again!
(Beat.)
AH! WE SHOULD PLAY DOMINOES! OR CHINESE CHECKERS!
Or, "CHINKERS CHECKERS" as I like to say. NO! Have you ever
played, "WAYS TO KILL BABIES?"
It's a miming game…and one person comes to the center…

(As Blanche DuBois.)

"No! I don't want the light…I want MAGIC!"

(A long pause.)

"Magic…." Funnily enough, that's the word Winston used to
describe my acting. Winston adores me, you know. He gave me a
painting he'd done just for me.
(Beat.)

What!? Winston Churchill. For fucks sake, what on Earth do they teach you in the American school system?

(A slight pause.)

Of course, Larry and I were in quite a lot together. But we've had our failures. I came up with the brilliant idea of investing his entire savings in taking Romeo and Juliet from London to Broadway. It was a complete flop. Darling Noel...Noel Coward...threw a party in New York at the time of the play, and when we arrived he said, "Darlings! How brave of you to come!"

(Beat.)

The critics said my voice was "too thin." But they always say that. Larry's reviews deemed his performance to be rather erratic, saying he sort of, "went off at half cock".

... twas ever thus....

All Larry cares about is work. Life is too short to work so hard. And all I really want is a good fuck!

You'd like another cigarette? Am I making you uncomfortable, darling? Good, because... to be quite honest dear, "your ladyship" is fucking bored with formality.

When I was a little girl and I was going to a party, my mother always said: "Now, do what the host wants, to please him." And when I was the hostess my mother used to say, "Now, do what the guests want, to please them." And I asked, "When can I do what I want to please ME?"

Not doing what you want is "good manners." I don't know about you, but I was raised on "good manners."

Of course, I do adore hosting. Larry and I have the best parties. Night after night I love seeing men in their dinner jackets...and women in their evening gowns.

Yes, I meet quite a few "casual lovers" at my events. I'm not sure where Larry finds his....but I do make mine known to him, quite obviously.

Well, if you're going to go to sleep every night at 8pm and ignore my offerings...what does he expect one to do?

(Beat.)

We do love each other, certainly.

(Beat.)

Lately, he and I are not…perhaps, as close as we would like, but he is preparing for his next role, which has been quite the distraction. He insists that in order to study the part he must "Explore the sexual life of the character" through the ever so tedious study of Sigmund Freud-and also, apparently, through committing the act of sodomy with Kenneth Tynan… the… drama critic.

I can see Kenneth now…sitting in his dungeon, writing and rewriting…slaving over the most hurtful reviews I've ever received.
(Beat.)
"Scarlett Capulet appeared this evening. She shakes her voice at the audience like a tiny fist."
"As Cleopatra, she picks at the part with the daintiness of a debutante called up to dismember a stag."
(Beat.)
But he always wrote that Larry's performances hit him…right below the belt.
(Beat.)
My mother told me, "Divorce is the ultimate sin. And you'll have to make your own peace with it." To sin again….
(Pause.)
Do you know what it's like to be loved? To be so truly loved. To have been with someone for so long…that everything and everyone else around you has been a blur…like
"you've kissed through centuries."
(Beat.)
No? Well…you're young. So very young, and beautiful.
(Beat.)
After lunch one day…in this very room. I told Larry I didn't love him anymore. I told him I loved him "like a brother, now."
"That's all."
Nothing works according to plan! You ought to be surprised in life. If not, it's a pity, I think.
Besides, I am thoroughly enjoying sex with Peter Finch. I must say, his cock is absolutely delightful!

(As Blanche DuBois.)
I've run for protection Stella, from one leaky roof to another leaky roof.

(Beat.)
But! Just look what happened! Larry came dashing half way across the world, braving all the cameras and the intrusive press, just to assure I returned to England safely…to make sure I was well. That is love.
(A slight pause.)
Have you heard of the actress Joan Plowright?
(Beat.)
No, well that's quite alright darling, no one really has. She's dreadfully ordinary. Like porridge or the color beige.

Joan Plowright….Plowright… I'd like to plow her rightly over the head with a shovel.

(Beat.)
Larry thinks my legs are too fat!
(Beat.)
Oh, you're too kind thank you.
I have always refused to dye my hair. My hair is very thin and dull, you see. I'm too afraid of the chemicals. But I made the sacrifice for Blanche, of course, of course, of course I did!
(Beat.)
AH! Yes! Blanche!
That is why you're here.
You want all my knowledge on Blanche to seep through my pores and into your little brain.
(Beat.)
You know when you're about to dive off a dock into the sea? There are some people who dip their toes in the water, testing the temperature; carefully prepping their arch as they contemplate the plunge…I…just…
DIVE!
And I swim! And I swim! And isn't it liberating when you swim!? When you're so deep in…you can't see anything below your …chest. To hell with precautions! Sometimes you have to leave someone behind because they're too damn "level headed" to enjoy anything!

My dearest friend in the whole world, Alan Dent, begged me not to do the role. I wouldn't hear it. It was impossible. I told him it was impossible. Absolutely no one could persuade me out of it.

Of course, I understand Blanche. You can't play her without understanding her. She is a tragic figure. But I'm not! I know where the divide is.

I am different from the roles I play. …When, when Scarlett wanted something out of life, she schemed about how to get it. That was her trouble. I just plunge ahead without thinking! That's my trouble!

(Beat.)

One thing about Scarlett… AND Blanche was exceptionally admirable. Their courage.

They had more than I'll ever have.

(Beat.)

My birth sign is Scorpio and they eat themselves up and burn themselves out. I swing between happiness and misery; I am part prude and part non-conformist.

Blanche never had sex for money! She had sex for love. Certainly, her sex drive was distressing…to some, but see, that amounted from a desperation for love. And everybody wants to be loved. What else is there? What will I do?

(Beat. She begins to sing.)

What'll I do-
When You-
Are Far Away-
And I'm-
So Blue-
What'll I do?

What'll I do-
With Just-
A Photograph.
To tell-
My Troubles
To.

When I'm Alone-
With Only-

Dreams of You-
That Wont-
Come True-
What'll I
(Beat.)

Have you read what they've been saying about me in the
"Hollywood Gutter Press?" That I go to the corners late at night and
bring home GOD knows whom. That I FUCK every sailor I meet?!
As if I'd ever.
And the taxi drivers....Well they were only because...

(As Blanche DuBois.)

"I never lied about anything! I never lied in my heart!"

I say what I feel and I don't pretend! I am prepared to accept the
consequences of my actions. I do not have some ridiculous "mental
illness."
I am adaptable.

Every truly talented actress must be able to adapt!
(Beat.)
But sometimes....I dread the truth of the lines.

(A slight pause.)

Marlon Brando practiced the "Method." I'm sure you're familiar
with that, being American.
(Beat.)
What was it like working with Marlon Brando? Hm, well do you
mean on or off set?
Either way, he worked tremendously hard. He was a novice when
it came to acting...and an expert when it came to fucking. The little
bugger fucks anything that moves, but heavens, is he good at it. If
only acting came as naturally to him as sex. I suppose he had his
methods for both. With some of the things he had me try it's a shock
I'm not seriously injured. But it was worth it, believe me.
Especially because I dread being alone in those rooms. I always
need something truly beautiful to look at in hotel rooms, whether it
be a Van Gogh hung... or Brando hung.

Ohhhh what a damn fool thing to say, forgive me.
Were they right? Was I mad to do it?

(Beat.)

I have almost a thousand pairs of white gloves!
(She gathers her gloves from a shelf.)

Aren't they beautiful? You see, I always hated my hands...I've been
told they're too big! Too thick! So...I wear these
gloves............What perfume do you wear?
(Beat.)
Never heard of it! This is "Belle Femme de la Nuit," but I call it
"Rape!"
My pearls! Oh good, I'm wearing my pearls. Sometimes I forget to
put them on which is terrible because my neck is as long as a
giraffe's!
Look at this darling gown! I got it as a gift from a lover in France.
There's only one in the whole world, and (She begins to cough) it's
mine!
(The cough grows worse.)
Please do forgive me for coughing, darling. I'm a tad ill, just a bit of
the Flu, I suspect. Some silly ass of a doctor told me I have some
dreadful condition but you know how doctors are, always making a
mountain out of a molehill! They want their money, yes they do.

(As Blanche DuBois.)

"Never has there been a light...brighter than this. Yellow lamp.
Gone...so quickly...how?"

(Beat.)
Everyone needs someone! Everyone. Everyone.

*(She makes her way over to the bar. Accidentally, she manages to spill a
glass of liquor on her dress as in "Streetcar Named Desire." Hurriedly, she
grabs a cloth and tries to clean it up. As Blanche DuBois.)*

"Right on my pretty...pretty......
Gently. *(She dabs.)* Gently.

No stain at all! You've got to shimmer and glow, shimmer and glow. Do you know what I mean? You've got to. I don't know how much longer I can turn the trick. It isn't enough to be soft. You've gotta be soft, and attractive…and I'm fading now.
(Beat.)
Have you been listening to me?
(Beat.)
I don't know why I screamed like that! I don't know why!
I want to rest…I want to breathe…quietly again. Just think, I can go away from here…and not be anyone's…problem."

(The phone rings.)

I am so terribly sorry. Please excuse me, I have been awaiting a phone call.

(Beat.)
Peter! Yes, I'm very well how are you? Your wife? How's the baby? Good, good I'm so glad. Yes. Yes…about returning to Ceylon, I managed to find a perfect flight that would bring me back just a couple days before filming, so I think.
Yes……I'm listening…..
Why would you imagine such a thing?
(Beat.)
Oh. Well, who do I need to write to to apologize? I didn't mean…
Yes?
(Beat.)
 Elizabeth Taylor is taking it.
(Pause.)
(As Blanche DuBois.)
"GET OUT! GET OUT OF HERE QUICK BEFORE I START SCREAMING FIRE!!!!! GO!!!!"
(Beat.)
 No…No! Wait! I thought you were my admirer! My friend! Don't go! Don't go darling, stay! Stay and….we'll dance! We'll dance, we'll dance, we'll dance!!!!!
(Beat.)

(As Blanche DuBois.)
"I've always depended on the kindness of strangers."

(A coughing spell attacks her and she collapses to the floor.)
I don't need the help no, I am fine…I am fine…I AM FINE!!!!
I don't need a custodian.
(A slight pause.)
You want to do this? Yes, you want to be an ACTRESS.
A BIG TIME actress.
Well, reality is so ugly…. *(Beat.)*
And you're a damn fool.
You're nothing but a damn fool.

(Pause.)

You've met with THE Mrs. Laurence Olivier.

Aren't you lucky?

Yes, well ….isn't it glamorous?

Isn't it dazzling?

(Beat.)
(Honestly, she asks herself)

 Isn't it lovely?

(Lights fade.)

THE END

Happily Never Ever

Characters:

SNOW WHITE: The vaginaless wonder, 19
BEAUTY: The transparent lady, 45
CINDERELLA: The leather skinned woman, 13
LITTLE RED RIDING HOOD: The cannibal, 10
RAPUNZEL: The bearded lady, 35
ACTRESS: Indicates the dropping of character

Style:

The stage should be set up with a three main areas – a chair for
RAPUNZEL SR, a chair or block in the center for SNOW WHITE and a
block or a chair for LITTLE RED RIDING HOOD to climb on and over SL.
BEAUTY and CINDERELLA stand.

There should be no costume or props to indicate the change of
characters; their transitions should be done physically. The actor
should also not be worried about standing in the right spot for
certain transitions – as long as the character is coming through, this
is all right.

There are also sections where dialogue happens in a rapid manner.
Don't worry about physicalizing this clearly; there should be
confusion and murkiness during those parts, in order to blur the
lines between the women and their stories, indicating the greater
meaning, that all these women are one, and, essentially, have one
unifying struggle.

(THE ACTRESS walks in a circle three times, speaking and moving slowly at first but faster and faster until she becomes BEAUTY)

ACTRESS: Mirror mirror on the over the river and through the woods to Let down your hair hair hair mirror on the wall E my name is Rapunzel Rapunzel, let down your mirror mirror E my name is There are rules you know, Mirror mirror on the over the river and through the woods to Let down your hair hair hair mirror on the wall E my name is Rapunzel Rapunzel, let down your mirror mirror E my name is There are rules you know, Mirror mirror on the over the river and through the woods to Let down your hair hair hair mirror on the wall E my name is Rapunzel Rapunzel, let down your mirror mirror E my name is There are rules you know

BEAUTY: Rules to being a lady

SNOW WHITE: Mirror Mirror

CINDERELLA: C-my name is

LITTLE RED RIDING HOOD: Across a sea of

RAPUNZEL: Rapunzel was left for dead

SNOW WHITE: Who's the fairest of them all?

(RAPUNZEL sits in an old rocking chair. She smokes a cigar and has a bottle of whiskey on the floor next to her)

RAPUNZEL: So, you know the deal, right? They're getting rid of one of us, budget cuts and what have you. But we get one chance to tell our story. To convince you who deserves to stay. And who's gonna go. So. I guess I'll just dive right in here. Go ahead, laugh. Everybody does. It's funny, right? A woman with a beard. I mean, that's funny in any case, but I mean, you know who I am, right? Right? The Radiant Rapunzel with a beard of silky gold. That's just…priceless. It makes sense, right? I mean, I'm hairy. Get it? You can laugh, go ahead and laugh, I have a good sense of humor. I mean, my parents named me Rapunzel. That is not. Normal. It was either have a good sense of humor or I don't know, die.
I would always rather not die. Given the choices, anyway.

You've heard the stories, yeah? Rapunzel with her fair flowing hair, locked in a doorless tower, her hair escaping the lone window only when the evil witch called to her. There's so much wrong with that idea.

My mother was crazy. But then again, whose isn't? I'm glad I'm not a mother. Would have hated to lose my figure. And my mind. It's a good thing I have my good looks to get me by.

(CINDERELLA *stands, paces back and forth, skipping awkwardly to the Rhyme*)

CINDERELLA: E-my name is Ella
My husband's name is Ed
We live in England
And we sell Elephants
E-my name is Ella
My husband's name is Ed...gar
We live in....E-reland
And we sell...Eeeeeeeeagles
E- my name is Ella
Do you know that stupid game? It's like one of those jump rope games, you know? Like, what's your name? *(Asks an audience member's name, does the game with their name)* It's dumb, but whatever.
[Awkward pause]
I don't know how to start.
I've never spoken to you guys before. So I don't know how to start.

RAPUNZEL: When I was a child, I was normal. I mean, all except for the name, but that was my mother's fault. And even then, it didn't make much of a difference because I was beautiful. The exotic name suited by exotic beauty. I wasn't promised to a witch or anything like that, that part got added to the story later. But I was beautiful. That part's true. My mother was proud of me, the way mothers are. Supposed to be. She was proud of me. Other mothers looked at me with jealousy biting their eyes...my mother told me I was special. Like the sun.
I was the sun.

Then the hair started growing.
I remember the first time she saw it, forcing its way through my
skin, through my cheeks, my chin, my neck, cracking my skin, my
beautiful porcelain skin.
I remember…she grabbed me by the chin

MOM: You have something on your chin.
  What is that?
  Rapunzel, what is that on your face?

RAPUNZEL: Rubbing my face, rubbing it with her forefinger and
  thumb then her whole hand

MOM: What is that?
  Is that hair?
  Is that
  Oh God, oh GOD what is happening?

CINDERELLA: Um, okay.
  Okay.
  So.
  I dunno, when I was six, I had a porcelain doll. I remember her. I
  loved that stupid doll, Papa gave her to me. And I loved Papa.

LITTLE RED RIDING HOOD: Over the river and through the woods to
  grandmommy's house I go! I know the way in sun and rain or a
  across a sea of sno-OH!
  The first time
  was….

RAPUNZEL: She tried everything to stop it. Obsessed. That's the
  word, she was obsessed with it. My father never could grow a
  beard so…
  That's a joke.
  Do you know what it's like? To lose your glow, to lose your
  shine? My face became tangled in weeds, my hair became a rat's
  nest and my heart became a stone. My mother's hair turned dirty
  and gray and her eyes turned to stones laced with blood.
  It was she who took me to the top of the doorless tower and
  chained my leg to the window so I could not escape, so I may

starve to death. So she could protect me from the world. She said. That's what she said, so I could starve to death in order to be saved. Because the world could be so cruel.
Because I couldn't gather that from my own mother locking me in doorless tower. Lesson learned, Ma. Lesson learned.

LITTLE RED RIDING HOOD: Over the river and through the woods to grandmommy's house I go....
The first time I tasted blood.
The first time I tasted blood wasssssssssssssssssssssss

CINDERELLA: My name is Ella.
Just Ella. Short for nothing, long for nothing. Do you know what it means? You're gonna laugh when I tell you. Rapunzel said it to me and she laughed and laughed and blew rings of smoke in my face that stuck to my skin so I grabbed her cigar and put it out in her beard and everything smelled like my father's old jackets and burning hair.
Ella, just Ella, all by itself with no Cinders attached, means Bright Light.
Rapunzel got mad at me, that I put her cigar out in her beard, but that's why I did it.
Because I was mad at her.

Papa was a storyteller
Papa came back from one of his adventures to the land of the rising sun, where the air smells like hot water and silent screams. Hot water and silent screams, the scent always clung to his hair when he came back, and his pockets were always lumpy with a gift for me. His eyes were like water caught in the sun, always sparkling.

PAPA: Ella, I have a special gift for you

CINDERELLA: And he slipped his hand into his pocket and pulled out the most perfect doll. Beautiful.
Perfect.
Perfect.

PAPA: She is made of porcelain. Do you know what that means?

CINDERELLA: No, Papa. Porcelain?

PAPA: It means made with magic.
It is made by taking the clouds from the sky on a dry day and
rolling them together with wet sand. Then it is sprinkled with
moondust, which falls to the earth only once a month, at the
shedding of the old moon to the new. It's the Moon that shapes it,
that gives it this color, do you see?
It's very precious.
Just like you.

CINDERELLA: She glowed, she was so white. I could see her, even in
the dark. And on nights that were long and cold, I could look at
my doll and know I was looking at the moon that shone above my
Papa, wherever he was.

RAPUNZEL: Rapunzel Rapunzel
He said he said
Let down your hair
He said he said
Don't bother
Said my mother
Rapunzel's already dead.
You like it? I made it up. Didn't seem right that I didn't get a
nursery rhymes, all the other bitches seem to have one.
But I survived. Obviously. I didn't die.
I starved, don't get me wrong. I felt hunger bruise my stomach,
saw the bones sticking through my hands. I starved and starved.
My hair fell out of my head, my gums bled, all that stuff. But
what could I do but sit there and starve.
My father came looking for me on like the third day or something.
I could hear him, standing outside the tower, calling for
me...Rapunzel Rapunzel!
My voice was too weak to carry anything back
Rapunzel! Rapunzel!
There was nothing to even throw.
Rapunzel! Are you there!
Sounded like music.
Until one day his voice stopped calling. And then there was

nothing, nowhere.

I could see the sun from the window where I was chained by my ankle across the room. The sun I had supposedly looked like. It was way too bright.

But anyway, onto the survival portion of the story,

One day as I was lying there in my filth, a little woodland creature came to the window and sang to me.

Sike.

Actually I had got so thin, I slipped my foot through and left. That was that.

Ah well, Obviously, I survived.

SNOW WHITE: Mirror mirror on the wall
　　Who's the fairest of them all?
　　Who's the fairest of them all?
　　No, wait.
　　Who's the purest of them all.

BEAUTY: When I was a little girl, I had two strands of pigtails that
　　trailed down my back, over my shoulders and down my back.
　　Two thick ropes of shiny brown hair, chestnut hair. That's what
　　my father called it. Chestnut.
　　My father used to call me a princess and carry me on his back.
　　And I was a princess.
　　His princess.
　　The princess with the long brown hair
　　No
　　With the long chestnut hair.
　　But then my hair began to fall out of my head.
　　Strand by strand, thread by thread slipped from the braids and fell
　　like a nest at my feet. Slowly and then faster and faster the hair fell
　　from my head and landed at my feet and there was nothing I
　　could do to get it to stay.
　　It fell and fell until I couldn't braid it anymore because the gaps of
　　my white head would show through.
　　It fell and fell and fell until I couldn't touch it because the slightest
　　whisper of a movement meant adding to the nest, adding to the
　　pile at my feet.

And it wasn't just my head-hair, it was my eyebrow hair and then my lashes, my beautiful long thick black lashes, they all joined the piled until I was naked.

Completely nude of hair.

I saved every hair that fell from my body, each beautiful strand and wove a blanket for my father.

He did not approve.

My father did not approve.

Would anyone like some tea?

CINDERELLA: Magic.

I remember believing in magic.

I remember the day I realized magic doesn't exist.

Remember the day you learned you couldn't fly?

No matter how you tried, you couldn't unglue your feet from the ground, you couldn't jump without the fall crumpling your body, your ankles shattered against the hard, cold reality. And all the wishes on all the stars in the night sky didn't change that.

Do you remember that day?

The day the sky fell, crashing at your feet.

The day the floor fell in and my step-mother told me my father no longer existed.

My father no longer existed.

Papa was a storyteller. I never knew his stories were lies. Papa wouldn't lie to me, would never lie to me, not to me, not to his princess, not to his little girl.

But all the stories he told about magic and happy endings, they were all lies, weren't they?

THEY'RE ALL LIES.

The doll Papa got me broke that day. It fell. Underneath my foot.

I couldn't sleep with her around.

Even in the dark, she was too bright.

It wasn't my fault

LITTLE RED RIDING HOOD: Over the river and through the woods to Grandmommy's house I go, I know the way, in sun or in rain, or across a sea of sno-OH

The first time I tasted blood was

BEAUTY: My father.

My father used to sit me down from the age of two and tell me
Beauty, there are rules, you know. Rules to being a lady.
Rules to being a lady.
Rule number one:
A lady never reveals her secrets.

LITTLE RED RIDING HOOD: I know the way in sun or in rain, or across a
sea of sno-OH!
The first time I tasted blood…
The first time I…
Usually all I do is sing and dance and eat some human stuff. For
the show. But Beauty told me I should tell this part…even though
I never told before. She said…if I wanted to stay in the show.
She said if I wanted to stay in the show, I would tell.
Tell about the first time I tasted blood.

BEAUTY: Rule number two:
A lady must be beautiful or at least make the effort to be beautiful.
Everything a lady does should be flawlessly executed, as natural
as the wind whistling through the leaves in autumn, when it
carries the sun on its wing. And this is to be able to become a
wife, which so happens to be Rule number Three.

LITTLE RED RIDING HOOD: And I'd ask her, "Mommy, why don't you go
with me to grandmommy's house", and she did once. She put her
hat on and took my hand. I was so happy, finally, finally mommy
was coming with me. I tried showing her all my secrets, but she
didn't even look. She just grabbed my hand in her hand and we
marched straight ahead, straight through to grandmommy's
house and she didn't look at any of my secrets, didn't look at them
not even once. Her fingers felt like claws, like steel claws.

CINDERELLA: You'll know this part.
When my father died, my step-mother turned me into a servant
and banished me to the basement where I made my bed out of the
dust and grime that stuck to the air down there.
Cinderskin. Papa would have thought that was clever of me, to
call it that.

Papa loved words. That's why he named me Ella. Because I was Papa's bright light. That's why I don't care. I don't care what happened next, I don't care about my cinderskin, because without Papa in this world, there is no light. There is no light at all.

LITTLE RED RIDING HOOD: I have a hole inside of me, a deep, deep hole that is emptyemptyempty.
I loved grandmommy's treats. I couldn't eat enough of them, couldn't swallow them down fast enough. I needed more and more and more sweets and grandma always had them waiting for me. Always had more and more and more to give me. But there were never enough.
Mother's food tasted like yuck. It had no taste except for healthy. There was something else in grandmommy's food, something that Mother's didn't have. And I couldn't eat enough. There would be plate after plate of cookies and brownies and cakes and ice creams and breads filled with nuts and berries and they would all go into my mouth. But no matter how many, no matter how many no matter how full I would get, I had to have more, had to fill myself with them. But no matter how full they made me, I was never full. I was still empty.

CINDERELLA: I think my lungs must have turned black first, but how could I have noticed? It's just a theory, anyway, with what I coughed up, thick globs of gunk that I would wipe off on my clothes, thick globs of gunk that glistened like slugs and would dry like mud on my clothes.

LITTLE RED RIDING HOOD: Bodies are weird. They don't act right. Like, I was empty inside but I kept on eating and the more I ate the emptier I felt but the bigger my body got, which made Mother's mouth go thinner and her eyes squintier and my cloak is the only thing that hid me, that I could hide inside, wrap the fabric around me and disappear. It was the closest to having a hug when nobody was there.
And nobody ever was there.

CINDERELLA: The air was filled with the whispers of shadows that fell like veils across the room. And the whispers of the shadows must have wrapped themselves around my arms, wrapped themselves around my legs, engrained themselves inside my skin until they stuck to me like glue, shadows that hugged me and wouldn't let go. That makes sense, that it was the shadows, first, that started to darken me because I turned gray before I turned black. I turned gray, a kind of tint of gray that almost glowed around my skin. I thought it was just the dirt, but it was all over, not patchy. I thought it was just me not feeling well, like how complexions get bad when you're feeling under the weather, but I kept getting grayer and grayer, like clouds that slowly filled themselves with rain.

Then the dust must have layered themselves ontop of the shadows on my skin and became trapped there, acting like a layer of glue for the dirt and the ashes that would cover me whole, that would make me black as a starless night, black as my father's shoe polish, and just as thick, too, because my skin turned to leather, became weathered leather so that there are lines and cracks running through me, through my black skin, through the shadows that have engrained themselves into my skin.

My step-mother's eyes turned to slits when she looked at me. They turned to slits and her lips would snarl and I'm not sure why. Really not sure why. She saw me turn to black, saw me turn from pale to gray to black and it was all her fault. It was all her fault, she kept me locked in a basement talking to shadows, drawing with dust and breathing in grime. She heard me coughing up globs of myself and wiping them on me and saw my skin get tattooed with the shadows and all she could do was hide the blackness of her pupils with the slits of her eyes.

LITTLE RED RIDING HOOD: The first time I tasted blood was from a cut on my hand. Picking roses with the Wolf. He was very nice. He liked my cloak. Asked me where I got it and I told him Grandmommy made it for me. And he said Oh, that's nice, where does she live? And I said Over there.
Over there.
He told me to stray from the path, to pick some roses. Bright, juicy roses. I had never saw roses before, not even never heard of them-only knew of the soft, delicate wildflowers that grew outside

the window of my house, that decorated the trail on my way to grandmommy's house.

His lips curled and his hands were soft.

His hands were soft and warm and mine were small and empty.

He didn't warn me about the thorns.

Nobody warned me about the thorns.

I could feel his eyes dance over me, but I thought he was looking at my cloak. I picked roses, rose and rose and then PRICK blood.

"What a pretty red cloak you have"

The blood didn't go away, so I sucked at it and sucked at it because he told me to

What a pretty red cloak you have

And I sucked at it and sucked at it and it was salty rust and it burned my tongue and then he said

Open Wide

Open wide he said

Open wide and

my mind was screaming NO but my body was getting softer and doing things I didn't know it could do.

It won't hurt if you open wide.

Blood is a different color from red. It stained my red cloak and it smelled like how it tasted.

I didn't want for there to be blood. But there was. There was.

There was all over, blood that tasted like rotted roses.

And then even those cakes couldn't get me full.

My skin shrank, and my belly rumbled, desperate for food, for something, anything, to make it full.

And then I found it.

But my mother did not approve.

I peel the skin back slowly, delicately. You can cook it, but it tastes better raw.

Marinate the skin in the blood.

I know, it looks icky, but it's really not all that bad. And it's the only thing I can eat.

SNOW WHITE: I've been traveling in this show for fifteen years. It's never the same. Except that it's always the same. Fifteen years, I've felt the weight of each footstep tremble inside my skin. And now

they want to get rid of one of us. Because staring at freaks is going out of style, because it's something wrong to do.
Beauty doesn't think I should be in the show because I'm beautiful. Because I don't look deformed. Because I look beautiful.
And she isn't.

LITTLE RED RIDING HOOD: Now that I'm here, I don't never wanna leave. And they all say that one of us gotta leave, and I don't wanna. Mother can't look at me. Neither can Grandmommy. I miss them, but I like it here. You look at me here.

CINDERELLA: They want to get rid of Beauty because she's the grossest. Nobody likes to look at her. She's the biggest freak around. But I don't want them to get rid of her because she's the grossest. She's grosser than me. Much, much grosser than me. But you can't tell what's wrong with Snow White, which I guess isn't fair. Because if you can't see it, how do you know it exists? And I guess Beauty has a point, that Snow White is still pretty and it isn't fair that she gets to be so pretty while all the rest of us get to look ugly and wrong, because even Little Red Riding Hood has crazy eyes and a mouth tinged with blood, and they'd probably lock her away since she eats people and stuff.
I guess it really isn't fair that Snow White's not as much a freak as the rest of us.
I guess it really, really isn't.

BEAUTY: And rule number four is

SNOW WHITE: Mirror mirror on the wall

BEAUTY: Rule number four is

SNOW WHITE: Mirror Mirror

BEAUTY: Rulenumberfouris
A woman's job is to have babies. There is no other goal in her life. There should not be any other goal in her life, no other distractions keeping her from being unable to fulfill her role, to be able to be a mother. And in order to do that, a woman must attract a man, see Rule numbers Three and Two. And when she is

to be a mother, she must never reveal her secrets for she must appear flawless. A mother is a child's God and she must be worshipped, but she must earn the right to be worshipped, see rule number One.

Simple.

It should have been so simple.

SNOW WHITE: Mirror, Mirror, on the wall
Who's the purest of them all?
Who knew nothing of the world
And lived her life like a girl
As pure as the freshly fallen snow
I've forgotten the rest. Slipped from my memory when I wasn't looking. Has that ever happened to you, sir? Do you know what I mean, miss? Something you know you knew as well as the rhythm of your own beating heart that has just...disappeared? Well, maybe it will come back for a visit. Maybe it will come back. I've never had to finish it before. Usually just whisper the beginning...that's all anyone seems to know. But now I must tell me story, else I get kicked out of the show.
Tell my story. Nobody's ever wanted to hear it before.

BEAUTY: Anyhow, the flakes began after my hair fell out.
Flakes of my skin, falling off bit by bit, flake by flake crumbling off my body from every inch of my body, falling softly like snow at my feet until there was enough to make a snow man.
My skin sheds like a snake, but more often and worse, and every hour on the hour and the skin that comes back is transparent.
I'm transparent.
You can see right through me.
My body is transparent. I have nothing to hide behind.
Do you know what that means, sir? Would you like to see, ma'am? Wait, wait keep looking at me, let me see your eyes.
They look like fire dipped in rain, quivering like sweetened jelly.
See? The blue veins with the red blood running through them, interweaving like the threads of a tapestry to the center of my heart
nestled underneath my lungs

my intestines squirming beneath, like worms.
Have you ever seen a bowel move?
I am disgusting to look at
because I have nothing to hide behind.
I cannot be a woman.
Whoever said Beauty was only skin deep obviously doesn't know
what skin deep looks like.
If anybody's hungry, I have some crumpets right here.

SNOW WHITE: I don't look into mirrors anymore. They're full of
danger. Never know who's looking in the other side.
I haven't looked at the audience in thirteen years. I used to, used
to watch their eyes. Squint, tremble, narrow- which is different
from a squint- widen, twitch but none of them ever smiled. None
of them ever smiled at me. Most eyes pitied me.
But at least I'm safe here. I'm safe.

BEAUTY: I tried to be a lady. Even now, I try. I try to be a proper
woman, what my father would have wanted to see. But how can I
when…
One more tip before you go - don't bother visiting Snow White.
There's nothing to see. Literally. Honestly, I don't even know
why she's in this show. If I were a lesser person, I might say
something nasty, but I won't.
You're still going to go see her, aren't you? I can see it in your
eyes. The curiosity. It looks like noodles, little runny lines of
noodles criss crossing your pupils, you're still going to see her,
aren't you. She's not worth the price of admission.
Don't you believe me?
Don't you believe the see-through woman? If I take off my shawl,
you could see my brain working.
WAIT.
Just answer me this –

Do you know what it's like to live like me? Leaving a trail of skin
scales everywhere you go?   All I've ever wanted to be close to
someone, to be loved by someone, anyone. I was banished to a
castle to live with a monster because nobody else would look at
me. I lived with a monster, with a creature whose heart was made

of diamond, claws made of iron who would not even touch me.

SNOW WHITE: Sometimes, in the dead of night, I feel myself.
Feel my face and imagine, try to imagine what I may look like.
Run my finger up and down the bridge of my nose, all around my
face, outlining cheekbones, jaw line, eyebrows. Sometimes, I'm
afraid I can feel my skin changing, right underneath my fingertips,
turning into lava, melting off and I want to look in a mirror, but I
don't. I keep feeling my face, enjoying each crevice, each curve
and –
Nobody told me.
Nobody told me that there was supposed to me more.
I am missing a – [Silence]
Missing the most important – *[Silence]*
I have nothing but a block of skin and no way to let a man in.
She saw me through the mirror, saw my reflection and she knew.
She knew and she sent the prince. No apples, no poisoned combs
or deadly bodices, she only sent a prince. Because she knew, even
if I didn't. She knew, knew that I was wrong.

BEAUTY: All I've ever done is try, I've tried and tried and tried to get
someone, anyone to look at me, to see me, to see my soul inside of
me but they can't, you can't, YOU CAN'T EVEN SEE ME and I've
never been allowed to be a lady, a real, true lady, not a wife or a
mother, I've failed and I can't fail again, don't you understand me,
I can't fail again. Please, please look at me, please someone see
me, don't be afraid to see me, don't be afraid of me, it's just blood
and guts and please look at me LOOK AT ME.

SNOW WHITE: I always dreamed of a Prince. Of someone who would
share their hands with me. Who would touch my face and feel my
breath wet the back of their neck and let me take care of him,
make sure his mouth always smiled and brushed away his tears at
night and massaged the kinks out of his joints. I dreamed of
someone who would take care of me. I didn't realize it came with
a debt I could not pay.
He screamed at me. Yelled at me like it was my fault, my fault for
not being able to fit him, not being able to swallow him whole.
He yelled at me and I didn't understand why or what, I thought

that love was kissing and holding and feeling one another's heart beat the same rhythm but there was something more,

PRINCE CHARMING: You tricked me

SNOW WHITE: I'm sorry. I'm so sorry.

PRINCE CHARMING: You made me fall in love with you

SNOW WHITE: I'm sorry, I didn't mean to

(She stops talking. This lasts a full minute, where she struggles to say words but can't. She can't speak)

SNOW WHITE: I can't do this.
I can't tell you.
I can't tell you because every word hurts.
No.
Every words stings like an icy bee sting stuck deep in the soft part of your heart
Every word, every word, I swore I wouldn't hear his words but there they are, flickering inside like fireflies, they don't die and I carry them around with me and they're alive, they're still alive and
He called me the Freak
He called ME a Freak so can't you see?
Can't you see?
I HURT SO MUCH.
I HURT SO MUCH
And if I don't belong here…then I don't belong anywhere.
Please don't make me leave.
Can't you see?
I'm the Biggest Freak of them All.

THE END

Cheap Chicken

Brooklyn, NY. A sparse, impersonal room. A barely used generic basement office. A woman, MARGARET, *in her 30's (or, in any event: too old to be cute by age and appearance; definitely an adult). She may be of any ethnicity. She may have a trace of an accent (any accent) one could find in Brooklyn. She is dressed in clothes that aim to be proper and professional. A plain button down shirt, every button closed; a simple skirt that is slightly too big and hangs loosely on her hips; shoes that are more comfortable than fashionable or feminine. - The whole ensemble seems borrowed from different good-will places. Her hair is pulled back and orderly. She holds a manila file-folder. Awkwardly. She is at an interview. For a job. As the lights come up Margaret stands, poised to begin, poised to answer a question. She is holding on tightly to that manila folder.*

MARGARET: As you can see from my sheet, Compare Foods is where I shop.

Not because it's cheaper. No. They encourage you to compare, but they never come out ahead. The jam I like, the Bonne Maman, is 5.19 and if I get it at Key Food then it's only 3.49. If I compare that, by comparison, Compare Foods has the higher price. So, unless they're aiming for exactly that, unless that's what they're after, they lose.

I never get the jam I like at Compare Foods. I get other things. The things that, by comparison, let Compare Foods come out ahead. Like chicken… The chicken can be cheap. Which is why I sometimes I have chicken on my morning toast. Because it's cheaper than Bonne Maman. Chicken on toast is nutritious. The chicken is a bargain.

But you have to work for the cheap chicken.

No cheap chicken comes cheap. You have to put the time in to get the cheap chicken. You have to be on your toes. You have to be ready to run and grab it, the cheap chicken. If you're not a good runner, or if your time is valuable then it might be better not to pursue the cheap chicken at all… I don't know how valuable your time is, but my time on Sunday is only worth about as much as a bottle-cork….

(A brief pause)

I've done that too, stayed home and been a bottle cork.

Rufus told me once I should put my thumb into his beerbottle, so the fizz doesn't escape. He had accidentally opened one too many beers and I was there, so he asked me to be a cap for his beer… I did it… Cause there was nothing else to do. And Rufus' patience is short. It's better for everyone if I just keep my finger in his beer and shut up. He didn't want me to walk around, Rufus didn't, because the beer should stay in the ice-bucket and not be suffering the bumps a human walk would cause.

Rufus loves his beer. It's special DOGFISHHEAD beer. I buy it for him at Compare Foods. Although compared to the Compare, Dogfishhead beer would be cheaper at the MET FOOD. But if I buy it at the MET food, I have to walk it home and that's 4 blocks, Compare Foods is just next door. And Rufus said he's willing to pay 1.75 more for a sixpack, if the beer doesn't have to get walked so far. Rufus is very peculiar about his beer. He likes it a great deal…

I don't mind being a beer buyer and a beer cork for him. He is my brother. He's always been…. Once he pushed me off a swing. He said, "hold your arms out, let's see if you can do swing with no hands". I did it… because…well…I did it. And then, instead of pushing the board he pushed me off, and I fell into the dirt. I didn't cry. But I l looked at him and asked "Why?" He said: "I'm your brother. I know what's good for you." He's known what's good for me ever since…

Rufus likes chicken too. Not as much as he likes Dogfishhead, but well enough. When he yells: "Where's the protein?" I know he means the chicken. And I serve it to him. He doesn't know it's cheap chicken. He thinks it has a fancy price. But the fact that it's cheap, it gives me so much pleasure. And it's the one thing I'll never tell Rufus.

I won't.

It's my secret. That I know how to get cheap chicken is my only secret. Just that I could serve it and know it's a bargain, makes me so quietly proud. Do you understand? I like eating the white meat and knowing that everyone who bought chicken yesterday paid 6.99 for the lemon- roasted or the BBQ-roasted, while I only paid 2.99 – for the same thing. I like that Rufus is ignorant about chicken. Do you know what I mean? There is a small thing I care for, there's one thing I know, and Rufus is ignorant. And because he's ignorant he doesn't try to take it from me. It's MINE.

Rufus has a lot of things and I have this one thing.

Often he gives me a 20 dollar bill to get us dinner for the week and when I say it's not enough, he says: "Stretch it!" I can. But only if I get the cheap chicken. If I get the cheap chicken, then I can make cheap chicken soup and maybe one cheap chicken-salad sandwich, depending how much protein Rufus needs in one sitting. Rufus is so hungry and he has no patience. "Now means now." He says.

(Pause.)

We have a gas stove.

(Pause.)

The self-lighting mechanism doesn't work. It just clicks and clicks and clicks, but the flame doesn't come on. This affects all 4 burners now. Rufus says it's because I clean the stove too little. I think it's because I clean it too much…

I NEED matches to light the burners. So I've asked Rufus to bring me packets of matches whenever he goes to a bar, because I know they give those away for free at the entrance. And why buy when you can free-sample. That's another thing about the Compare Foods. They have no free-sampling. They do at the Met-food. Mostly cheese-bits and cracker-crumbs, but I can make a meal of that. Especially when the manager lets me keep a split tomato. On Thursdays Rufus brings me matches from the "Staghorn." I don't know what it looks like there, but according to the matchbook it's elegant. And not too cheap. They probably have Dogfishhead beer on tap. When Rufus comes home happy from "kissing the Dogfishhead", he brings me matches. For the stove. Only for the stove. "Don't play with the matches!" he says.

I keep the match-books in an empty blackbean-can. That the matches are only for the stove, I know that.

(Pause.)

I don't know why I held a burning match to Rufus' sleeve that Sunday.

He was asleep from 5 Dogfishheads. He was asleep, his mouth was a little open, he looked soft, and I knelt down by his side and I lit him. I don't know why.

It was a Sunday, I was happy I had gotten the cheap chicken and the evening was an evening like all evenings, really, but suddenly I thought of putting the match to Rufus. No, I didn't think that. I just did it. I held a match to Rufus…

I was curious.

(Pause.)

POW. Like the stove. Pow. There were flames. It burst into flame, his shirt. Right away. It wasn't a retardant material. It wasn't.

Not like I am. I am retardant material. Retardant means "slow to catch on fire." That's me. Rufus told me I'm retardant. But his shirt wasn't that. It burst into flames. It melted into his skin. It fused with him – "beyond recognition." He was "beyond recognition." I didn't recognize the sounds he made when he was in flames. The smoke alarm went off. I was surprised to hear it. No-one replaces the batteries and we've lived here so long.

Rufus' skin peeled off his cheek. It smelled like tires and cheap chicken.

I stood still.
Rufus put himself out then. Threw himself onto the floor. Flapping. Rolling. Screaming.

I stood still.

Someone must have called authorities. An authority broke down the door. I stood in the kitchen corner still holding the Staghorn matchbook. Rufus whimpered on the checkered floor. The authority yelled at me. "He's my brother." I said but they wanted me to come with them. I did. I didn't take anything except a grocery-bag with the leftover cheap chicken. The authority let me. Because of my psychology, I think.

(Pause.)

Rufus doesn't look like Rufus. He lost one eye. One entire side. I've seen a picture. I wasn't supposed to see it but it was an accessory to a file with my name.

They have separated us. We are not allowed contact.

(Pause.)

Oh! My psychology has been evaluated. I am not dangerous.

I have a place at the Common Living Center. I made a friend there. Marlene. She's my roommate and she's quiet. She drinks 7-up. I've offered to be her bottle-cork, but she says, she's not concerned about flat lemonade. It's the conspiracies that concern her. How the government systematically poisons our drinking water. Which is why she drinks bottled soda. She gets a quick flicker in her eyes when she speaks of conspiracies. I can tell she'd like to talk more about that, but she gets tired quickly.

Overall she's gentle, Marlene is. So gentle. She saved a spider and a ladybug under a glass and then set them free. She doesn't step on any living thing. I like her ...so much...

Last night I told her, after lights out, I told her about Compare Foods. I whispered: "Marlene?...Marlene!! You have to meander by the baked goods. Look at the raisin bread like it's very interesting, you have to meander by the baguettes between 8 and 8:15 pm. And you have to listen, Marlene. Because suddenly around between 8 and 8:15 pm there will be a voice on the loudspeaker and they'll announce that any left-over roasted chicken is on special sale this last hour before closing. They'll yell: "2.99!"... Only 2 dollars and 99 cents!! That's when you have to run. RUN for the chicken shelf. A lot of people in the store will be running for it too, but if you're at the baked goods then you'll have a head-start! It's easy. You have to know it's coming. And be prepared. But when you get it, there's nothing like a cheap chicken."

She reached for my hand across the nightstand then, and I took hers. I like her...so much.

(Pause. She searches. Then a breath.)

That's all there is about me.

(Pause.)

Is that what you meant when you said: "Tell me about yourself?" Have I said enough? I never know...

I have a place to live until Winter, with meals and Marlene. I know about shopping. I know about groceries. I've shopped at the Met Food, the Key Food and the Compare Foods. I can sweep. I can sticker the pears and oranges. I can stock the Bonne Maman, which , I think, you price at 3.89 – that's good.

(She opens her folder and reads from a statement she has prepared.)

"I want to take this on, because I'd like to independently steady myself. I'd like to get some solidity..." *(She closes the folder, looks up)*

...and get a studio in Brighton Beach -it's affordable there Marlene says, and then I'd like to ask Marlene to live with me in the hours between work. That's the goal!

Is that what you meant when you said "Tell me about yourself. Tell me about your goals?" Is that what you meant? I never know.

I could do a good job for you and the Emporium. I am a good helper. I know that.

(She stands. There is nothing else to say. She looks and waits for a response. Until the lights fade.)

THE END

Out of My Mind

Lights up on a woman sitting in a chair, palms resting on her thighs, eyes closed. She opens her eyes, looks intently at someone in the midst of the audience.

"Kiss me. Kiss me. I know I'm married, but just kiss me, because I can't kiss you. But, I'll kiss you back, just for a minute, and we can do that and I can feel it, the thrill, the something. Just, kiss me."

She closes her eyes. She opens them, stands.

The summer I was 16, I went away to a summer theatre program at Northwestern University. And, I loved it. I loved getting away and reinventing myself, being surrounded by theatre geeks, and getting to know the other Cherubs, as we were called. I was finding my way, my niche; I really liked the Chicagoans, the Midwesterners, and, of course, I understood the west coast kids, and even the southerners, but the east coast kids eluded me. *(confesses)* They intimidated me. It's like the other day: I got off the R train at 23rd and, almost upon surfacing, I thought "wow, this neighborhood is way cooler than me." I actually said it out loud, further proving that the Flatiron is, indeed, way cooler than I am. And when I was sixteen, I knew that about the New Yorkers: they were way cooler than I was.

In the program, we all took acting, and voice, and movement, and had a choice of two electives. I knew I wanted to study dialects because *(in an accent)* I'd always been good at accents, but was at a loss for the second class. This skinny girl from Manhattan with an impressive vocabulary, who wore equally skinny Earl Jeans, a brand with which I feigned familiarity, said that her friend said that Energy Awareness was cool. *(shrugs)* So, I signed up.

When I was a kid, I, like many children, imagined I was someone else.... I imagined I lived in the country and had a horse, or was an orphan and lived like The Boxcar Children, or was a runaway. But, I never, never, ran away; I never even threatened to run away, I never packed a bag.

My daughter's in kindergarten and they have all these conferences and assessments, and she's a good student. She is a good little student, because she internalizes expectations. She takes the school's expectations of her and she makes them her own. She gets in line, because she wants to get in line. I internalize expectations. I would never have run away, I don't run away, because I'm expected to stay. I expect it of myself. It doesn't mean I don't fantasize about running away -- even now -- a different circumstance...Autonomy.

Pause.

On the first day of Energy Awareness, our teacher, a geeky, thin man who tucked his t-shirt firmly into high-waisted snug pants, showed us his visualization collage. This was a piece of red construction paper with magazine cutout pictures of the character Luke from the duo Luke and Laura from General Hospital pasted to it in a kind of a Candyland swirl pattern. This chart, he explained, would help him attain his life goal of being on a soap opera. Now, letting alone the whole notion of a visualization collage, I thought his life goal seemed utterly ridiculous; my life goal, at sixteen, was to be the next Dustin Hoffman. Besides, I'd been raised without a television -- the only time I'd ever seen a soap opera was when I was in the hospital at fifteen, recovering from an appendectomy. I remember looking up at the screen confused when I heard "Gone, dreams of the past, Gone, with a love that moved too fast." Why was my audition song playing over the credits for The Young and Restless? "Gone, bright shiny days, Gone in a young and restless haze" Oh, I was so gauche! And, meanwhile, who recommended that song to a twelve year old? So, I thought my teacher's goal was silly and the appendectomy was not a great association, but I was a teenager and an actor in a classroom full of teenage actors, misfits on the surface or down deep, and we put our heads down and saved our comments for after class.

In labor – don't worry, I'm not going to subject you to the details of my childbirth experience, for all our sakes -- but, during labor, *(lying down on her side)* if you give over, let the animal brain or hormones or whatever take over, you actually fall asleep between contractions. You leave the room for three minutes. You float away.

I'm fairly certain this only happens to those of us who make the whacky choice to have a "natural" childbirth. I know, we all have our reasons and, yeah, I figured it'd be better for the kid if I weren't on drugs, but really, I did it to do it. I just wanted to have a human experience, to feel it. And I did. But what stays with me, what I really remember, is that three minute shut down, lying there asleep with my eyes open, the bare trees of central park in blurry soft focus, all my muscles slack, the breathing effortless, the smell of the Balance Bar my second husband is shoving in his mouth. "You're eating?" *(pause)* "You're eating?!!" That I remember.

(Sitting up) They say that you don't remember the pain, but you do. You do. I was much less committed to "natural" child birth the second time around, but I said I'd do it, and…it's kind of like war, once you're in the shit, you're in the shit.

Pause. She stands.

Energy Awareness is basically about being aware of your energy. Our teacher showed us how much energy we waste brushing our hair like this, instead of like this *(demonstrates stress-full and stress-free brushing)*. And, to this day I strive to brush my teeth with as little wasted energy as possible. We spent classes rooting ourselves to the center of the earth, connecting with the energy of the universe, and cleansing our chakras. My classmates and I were skeptical, but we were game. There was an unspoken understanding, though, a line you didn't cross: giving backrubs was cool, speaking in tongues was not. Auras were sexy, animal spirit guides were not. And at sixteen, it's all about sexy.

Speaking of…auras, the aura fluffing exercise was a class favorite. One student would stand in the middle of the room, surrounded by fluffers – yes, fluffers -- and we would fluff the student in the middle's aura. *(starts fluffing)* As we fluffed, our teacher would encourage us to notice where the energy gathered and which chakras were blocked. This was foreplay: an opportunity to lay the groundwork for a move at the next dance party. A cute guy's energy inevitably gathered around the Base chakra;, and a hot girl always had great heart energy. *(stops fluffing)* When I got my aura fluffed, everyone said my energy gathered in my crown chakra, the top of my head. Anyway.

She sits on chair, eyes closed. Pause. She opens them, looks at an imagined someone in the audience.

"Kiss me. Kiss me." I used to will my scene partner, a slightly doughy almost good looking boy from the south who would have held little appeal had I not felt so trapped, to kiss me, take me against my will, because of my will. "Kiss me. Kiss me. I know I'm married, but just kiss me, because I can't kiss you. But, I'll kiss you back just for a minute and we can do that and I can feel it, the thrill, the something. I want to be that girl. Just, kiss me." *(pause)* I got that kind of kiss once, the transportive kind. Well before I was ever married. On the last day of college, Jason Freitag took me out by the trash cans at a house party, dipped me back, kissed me, and said: "Now you know why I always said we'd make a great sitcom couple. It wasn't just because we'd be funny." That boy could have taken me anywhere. I don't know if it was the beer, or the kiss – which was excellent – but, I mean, name your desert island. He didn't. He was drunk and seemingly didn't remember any of it later. And that's it. That is my Hollywood fairytale screen kiss -- swept off my feet next to the dumpster by a dude who would deny it ever happened. But, for a moment, it was romance.

I come from a family that was longer on cynicism than spirituality; the bible shared a bookshelf with Marx, and New Age bullshit was just that. But, my childhood in Northern California, home of the healing crystal, where traffic jams are blamed on – no, really, caused – by Mercury in retrograde, gave me an advantage of sorts over my classmates from Akron, Ohio. But, even I was skeptical when the day came for us to leave our bodies.

Our teacher -- I keep wanting to call him Luke, but I think that's just because of his visualization collage -- described leaving your body as the ultimate peaceful experience, that there was nothing like floating on the ceiling looking down at your body lying below. The class wasn't buying it, but we played along, figured we'd go through the motions. He had us put our chairs in a circle facing each other, sit up straight, put our feet flat on the ground, place our palms on our thighs, close our eyes, and let our crown chakras open. *(She does it, screams instantly, and slaps her hands on her head.)* The minute, no, the second, the moment I assumed the position, I felt the top of my head start to open up like a spiral vegetable strainer, like an alien ship and I shrieked and clapped both of my hands over my head. Luke told everyone to keep their eyes closed, to concentrate on their own experiences, but I'm sure they peeked, wondered whether I was freakish enough to think I was actually going to leave my body right there in Room 102, or assumed I was making a sad little try for attention. But I didn't care, I just kept my hands on my head to keep whatever was in there, in there, and explained to Luke, or whatever his name was, that "my head is splitting open." He told me just to relax and embrace the experience. *(She goes through the motions again, her head splits open. She shrieks.)* Not cool. Not sexy.

It was months before I could sit upright in a chair and not feel my head split open. I didn't even have to close my eyes. And, for a while, I was afraid that I'd be plagued forever like those women who have spontaneous orgasms after being burned by coffee at McDonald's. But now, it never happens, even when I try.

Sits on chair, closes eyes. It doesn't work.

Someone did kiss me, when I was married, and I tried not to kiss him back. I tried. *(pause)* It was a kiss, but it felt like love, like cupid's hormone arrow coursing through my veins, taking over, interrupting my sleep, stealing my appetite. And I didn't feel like myself. Or, I did -- I felt more like myself. I felt like myself on steroids, I felt like myself on estrogen, no testosterone. And all I know is that I want it, I want it like Romeo and Juliet want it – not double suicide, but climb up your balcony, sneak out your window, adolescent total disregard for decorum want it, want this love drug that I am making. Maybe I've been laboring under this misconception that I have any control at all, that I can keep whatever's in there, in there, because it is shooting out all over the place.

And, I am walking down the street and the sun is shining and I notice my legs as if for the first time, and I notice my gait and my posture – the shoulders back and relaxed, which never happened before despite all the yoga and t'ai chi. And the air comes in so easily that it makes me light headed, and my thighs rubbing together make me feel excited, instead of just making me want to diet. I remember this girl, I know this body. Where did it…? *(interrupts herself)* Eh, it doesn't matter – it's back! And the sun is shining, and my legs are rubbing, and men are smiling…

Pause.

The other night my daughter had trouble falling asleep; internalizing all those expectations can stress you out. Now, I don't know how many of you have ever tried to get a six year-old who thinks she can't sleep just to lie down, but it is a challenge. Somehow, though, through the miracle of mommy magic, I get her to lie down, and I decide to lead her on a visualization exercise. I start with "close your eyes," "I can't close my eyes," "okay, just relax your face," "I can't relax my face!" "Okay, well then just let your body be still" "I can't be still, Mom, that's why I need you to do the thing!" "I'm doing it, this is the thing, this is the thing." I'm starting to lose confidence in the entire undertaking, "Okay, don't worry about your eyes or your face, or relaxing or being still, just breathe, just breathe." And then I take her through the relaxation exercise, "Now, on your next breath, you notice that your feet feel heavy, so heavy they could pass right through your bed, through our building and come to rest on the earth below…" I go through every body part this way until her whole body is resting perfectly supported on a bed of leaves. And, I'm feeling pretty wiped out at this point and I close my eyes and I imagine what it would feel like to be perfectly supported by a bed of leaves. "…and with your next breath all your tension leaves your body and you feel yourself getting lighter, and lighter, so light that you start to float through the air…" I open my eyes to check on her and she is *(jumps up on chair)* out of her covers, on top of her bed, going like this *(arms outstretched, floating on the breeze)*. And, she looks at me, and says, "I don't know what I'm supposed to be doing." And I say, "Are you trying to float?" And
she says, "Yes."

She hops down, looks at the audience.

Yes!

THE END

Octopus

It is a glowy sort of dish.

Hacked up, boiled, drowned in olive oil, lemon, and an abusive amount of garlic; the flesh as multi-colored as a Mediterranean sunset, tentacles curling delicately, suckers erect. Every Italian youngster eats her first bite on a dare, and is forever lost to the joys of the thing. Converted to savagery.
Octopus is a notoriously beautiful creature. It is notoriously difficult to clean and cook.

I know I will never make a decent polpo, myself. I tried it once. There are a few things more disgusting than a freshly dead cephalopod, but I've never had any of them in my kitchen. In water, the octopus is a muscular miracle of grace. In my sink, it is a viscous, membranous mess. In my pot it puffs up, goes purple, boils down and turns into a tire.
My Sicilian ancestors would tenderize an octopus by hurling it against a stone until it was exhausted.
I lack the stones.

No amount of lemon and garlic can make this edible.

No amount of verbal gymnastics here can convey to you the taste and texture of my grandmother's octopus. The sort of jockeying at table that I and my brother employ, inflicting fork wounds on one another's knuckles as we dive for our fair share.

I am seven, eight, nine, ten, mute as a mollusk and shocked every year when Dad suggests I speak a prayer before dinner.
We only get octopus at Christmas. I am only ever called upon to pray on Christmas Eve.
We are not a pious family, aside from Grandma, who is easily the meanest of us, so I am always unprepared.
My father asks for a prayer, and inevitably, although I know the request is coming, I have no prayer for him.

I go to Catholic Sunday School just long enough to develop the requisite fascination with torture and to draw idle pictures of Pontius Pilate in a bi-plane, and then my mother yanks me out with

as little explanation as I had going into the thing. I respect her decision, primarily because I can now go back to watching Mighty Mouse cartoons of a Sunday morning, but as a result, I have no easy canned prayers available, in the event of food, or death, or any of the less compelling chapters in between.
This will eventually cause me trouble.

For now, I consider an extemporaneous communication with the greatest Italian of them all. (At this point I imagine Christ lives in the Vatican.)

God?

Signore...?

I wish *I* were an octopus, right now.
Not the one on the table.
One of those poisonous little blue ones from Australia; they're itty-bitty and they're lethal. They sting you and you're paralyzed, right, and you're absolutely aware of everything going on around you and inside you, but you're unable to move as you
slowly slowly slowly
slowly slowly slowly
slowly
die.
Like the blue in my mom's middle distance gaze.

But I reject this prayer. It would require explanation, which would be time consuming and inappropriate.

I go instead with something I heard on Romper Room-
godisgreatgodisgoodletusthankhimforourfoodamen.
Mom is thin and my dad is good lookin' "So hush little baby, don't you cry."

God my mom is skinny! Dad procured her fresh from an Idaho dairy farm, a non-Italian ectomorph in the extreme: freckled, fair, nervous as a guppy.
I know he got her in his car and proposed to her while he was driving 90 miles an hour down a late night highway. Mom told him; no, she would not marry him, and he threatened to drive

faster until she said yes.

Under the threat of vehicular manslaughter, marriage took on a new glow.

He presented her to his mother, who sighed and said "Sam, you used to date such pretty girls!" She then went about teaching my mom how to make a sauce.

I know I will never taste a spaghetti sauce like my grandmother's again. She put hardboiled eggs and neck bones in her sauce, which gave it a carnal meaty heft. She tried to teach her daughter in law, the shit kicker, how to accomplish it.

But no two cooks, even if they're both Sicilian, can make the same sauce.

Even if they were to use the same ingredients in the same measurements (which they never do, it is always a "pinch" of sugar to cut the acidity of the tomatoes, a "splash" of olive oil to bind it, and, hilariously, "some" garlic) even so, the two pots will always be different, will always reflect the personality of the creator.

Mom's sauce turned out thin, but intriguing and autumnal, with a kick not of shit, but of nutmeg.

I make a sauce too. It is not my mother's sauce. It is not my grandmother's sauce. Neither lady ever taught me how to make a sauce. I got mine from a book.

Dad gets his ideas about how to be Italian from books, as well.

Dad wishes to be a Wiseguy.

Dad has a close relationship with Mario Puzo, but Mario doesn't know it.

Dad doesn't wear his wedding ring. He has a diamond pinkie ring, and a gold nugget ring with diamond chips, and a gold wristwatch. His gold Italian horn necklace is decorated with an engraving of a woman's face, like a mermaid on the prow of a ship; all of it is Italian gold, which we are given to understand is better quality than any other sort of gold. We keep a jar of hot giardiniera in the fridge for him, and every Sunday and Wednesday he anoints his pasta with it as though baptizing an infidel, and the heat from the peppers makes him sweat over his supper. He wears VO5 in his black hair and he keeps two guns in a shoe box on the high shelf of his walk in closet, next to a pile of Penthouse magazines. His restaurant is called Villa D'Oro and his mistress is a red head, and both of them are in Des Plaines.

He wants glamour, you know, and money. Drama at no cost.

He settles for Villa D'Oro, which means Village of Gold, but it's not Italian gold, you know, it's really just Des Plaines.

Maybe when he urges me to pray, he means I should pray I never end up in Des Plaines.

Presiding over a minefield of white table clothes and a morbidly obese cook named, (of course) Tiny. My mom works an office job all day and waits on the tables at night. My dad arranges for fashion shows featuring lingerie models during the businessmen's lunches. Behind the bar, he switches the Makers Mark out of its bottle and replaces it with cheap bourbon, and when the electric is cut off because he hasn't paid the bill, he lights the candles on the tables and tells the customers that there is a power outage, even though the customers and my father can plainly see the rest of Des Plaines sparkling like a fairy tale through the big windows. As bold a liar as any elected official, Dad sticks to his story in spite of the facts, and continues to present rapidly cooling plates of spaghetti drowned in Tiny's signature marinara.

Tiny makes this really wretched marinara sauce which I refuse to eat, recognizing at an early age that my Grandmother's cooking is superior and wondering why my father runs a restaurant where the food can't hope to compare to his mother's kitchen. In the afternoons, when there are no customers, I sit under a table in a tablecloth tent, and color. Dad lets me wash the glasses in the bar. There is a rubber mat on the floor, in case I drop one.

Sometimes when the phone rings, at Villa D'oro, Dad answers, listens a moment, and says, "Yes, we have meatballs."
My mother knows that this is code for "my wife is here, you can't come sit in the bar."

I know Mom was once arrested for loitering suspiciously around the bushes of a Des Plaines motel while trying to catch Dad and his Puttana in the act.

I know how to make a puttanesca.   I learned it from a book

It is so named because it's the sort of meal a whore could whip up in no time, between clients or perhaps with a favorite. Olive oil and anchovies are the basis. It is a sauce for grown-ups; for sexual encounters, aphrodisiac and appalling, clotted with barely dissolved tomatoes, sweating salt from our Greek friends the kalamatas, and shot through with brine from the capers. It is not meant to be served over spaghetti. You eat it with penne, the tube shaped pasta so handy for scooping up your sweatier sauces.
Lots of bread.
A lover, because the anchovies have demonstrated how to dissolve in heat and the oil leaves your mouth slick and since you've both eaten it, the garlic will offend no one.

It is after hours at Villa D'oro, the chairs up on the tables, the lights dim, when my mother's chronic, hot humiliation finally boils over into a classic rage and she suddenly goes all Italian. Her rage is operatic. She howls and hammers, she tears white clothes from the tables, she breaks the dishes, she smashes the cheap hooch.
He slaps her to the floor, kicks her in the ribs, and opens the side of her head.
It does not hurt a lick, until the next day, of course.

It is a decade later when I think to I ask her if it was worth it. She smiles with all the dirt farmer glee of her Tennessee tobacco ancestors, yes; but there are also some hardboiled eggs and neckbones in that sauce.

Meanwhile the octopus, as we know, shoots ink in order to confuse its enemies.

Interesting fact: if it is trapped in an enclosed space such as an underwater cave, or a tank, the ink will fail to disperse, turn toxic, and kill it.

I am so pregnant when I come flying into the hospital on that frozen February 3 a.m., the security officer in the lobby springs up and cries, "Okay then!" and hustles to get me a wheelchair.
I don't stop for him.

I would have to explain to him that I am not in labor; that I am on my way up to intensive care, to see my father, who'd suffered cardiac arrest.

I would have to explain to him that I didn't know what cardiac arrest meant when the nurse called me an hour before, and I told her, stupidly, that I would come by in the morning.

I would have to explain to him how my husband urged me not to go to this deathwatch.

How romantic bedside father/daughter reconciliations do not take place when the husband must first shovel the car out of two feet of snow and place his exhausted, ambivalent, pregnant wife behind the wheel, unable to accompany her because they are both unwilling to wake their toddler daughter so that she may be a witness to it all. He stays home with the sleeping child. I am here, kind security officer, because I don't want to be yelled at by my Grandmother. I don't want to have to face my grandmother at the funeral home the next day with the confession that I'd been waiting for this a long time and have no stake in seeing the old man's evacuated body at the hospital at 3 in the morning. I am here because I feel like I have to be.

I do not explain all this to the helpful security officer in the lobby.

I can't tell him some of it, without admitting to all of it, and that would be time consuming and inappropriate.

Can't stop, not having baby, just visiting!
godisgreatgodisgoodletusthankhimforourfoodamen!

and I make my way through the Byzantine disorder of corridors known as Resurrection Hospital.
Resurrection. God Forbid.
"Can't stop, not having baby, just visiting?"

Moron.

Why is it so important to me to pretend everything is all right? It's a fucking hospital. At fucking three o'clock in the morning. Who is going to suspect anything is other than terribly not all right? Why should I care? Someone just died. People are dying all over this hospital. I trundle through it, carrying two sons within me. Life and Death and my concern is that any passing intern will assume my shit is sufficiently together.

He is a mess, A bag of soft tissue hurled against a rock to exhaustion. Skin laid sloppy over bone. As multi colored as a Mediterranean sunset. Eyelids caving in, mouth open and so strange when not in use
Lifeless, wifeless, purple tinged, boiled dry, and I am the only family here in the ICU, and as usual I have no prayer for him.

At his funeral I stand next to his coffin, holding my toddler daughter in my arms.
"So long, Sam."

Not many people will attend his funeral, and those who do will go to an Italian restaurant afterwards for pretty bad pasta and a chance to see my daughter throw her fusilli the length of the table. She will never know her grandfather.

A year before his death, I took her to visit him. He was ill with radiation (prostate cancer) and weak. She was twelve months old and a sharp, quizzical bird of a thing, hard where you expect her to be soft and vice versa. She played with his hooked nose. He said, quietly, "She makes me laugh." I felt like he had finally looked at someone other than himself and really seen her. His grand-daughter; not a soft cooing ornamental baby, but an inquisitive force of nature, and a humorous one.

Likewise I came to see him in intensive care, a week before he died. Bulging and uncomfortable (there is no place to sit in ICU) I told him I was expecting twins.

Again, he smiled, but not for show. His smiles used to be one of two things- disingenuous or shark-like. From his hospital bed, beneath the oxygen tubes, his smile was directed inward, as was his comment.

"You always have to do things differently, don't you?"

I don't know the name of the graveyard where he is buried. I find my way there four months after he dies, with my sister, from whom he'd been estranged. She wants to see his grave and hash a few things out with him. I give her her privacy. My daughter and I wander the cemetery and I explain the dead people to her.

When my sister finishes, it's my turn.

I stand by Dad's grave and search around for something to say.

As usual, we don't have much in common to talk about.

As usual, the whole scenario embarrasses me.

As usual, I don't have a prayer.

My daughter plays among the graves; rearranging the various floral displays left by loved ones there and stealing a small Virgin Mary.

THE END

I You're Feeling Blue, Paint Yourself a Different Color!

(Bright.)

I would like to be joyous and celebratory but I end up spitting toothpaste into the sink and obsessing over the strange new wrinkles on the bridge of my nose while my husband sits fully naked on the toilet.

My husband fully naked is a joyous and celebratory thing: aesthetically, sexually and sometimes comically satisfying, but he is on the toilet right now and I'm not here to celebrate his processes of elimination any more than I would worship at the altar of the Goddess of Menstruation. I'm happy we function, but I'm not mystical about it.

My husband and I have an unspoken rule: we may pee in front of each other but defecation is best done in private. He is not defecating. He is peeing. He sometimes sits to pee, which I find endearing, it's much less aggressive than the typical male stance; spread apart, taking aim and taking cover all at once, presenting the world with back and buttocks. When he sits, it is because he is tired, but he is fastidious; with one finger he gently pushes his penis down so that he will urinate directly into the toilet and make no splash.

He is a very delightful man.

When he sits like this, we can have a conversation, and our conversation meanders through the schedule of the coming week and around groceries and over car maintenance and he mentions an article he read about Palestine and I steer him away from it because I don't want to talk about the middle east, I want to talk about an imagined slight I received at the hands of one of the other neighborhood moms, a PTO lady, and how much I hate the PTO ladies and that reminds me of a dream I had

(abrupt light change)

where there was this flying saucer, very old fashioned but very ominous threatening the Eisenhower and a bunch of us abandoned our cars and were hiding in the shadow of an overpass and one of the PTO ladies I happened to be with decided that since I wasn't on the PTO I shouldn't be taking up valuable hiding space and she was very snarky about me thinking I was some sort of "writer" and she attempted to sodomize me with a fountain pen the size of a golf umbrella.

(*Restore light*)

And somewhere in this conversation my husband and I come to a shared conclusion and this ladies and gentlemen, is why the marriage has lasted as long as it has- the shared conclusion we reach is that there are two things in this life that neither of us fully understand.

The first is the impulse to defecate on top of your partner during sex. An act sometimes described as a Cleveland Steamer.

The second is scrapbooking. Only ever described as scrapbooking.

For those of you who have never encountered true scrapbooking, who have never set foot in a Michaels or a Joanne's Fabrics, rest assured I am not talking about simply tearing an article from a newspaper and slapping it into an album for safekeeping. I'm talking about a consecrated book the size of the Riverside Shakespeare,
With Pages of flesh toned vellum

(*start a slow light shift to something sexy*)

Textured hemp
Stiffened velvet in stone fruit shades of plum, peach, nectarine
Silks and grosgrain ribbon
three different types of scissors required
Cords of leather and buttons of pearl and pots of mucilage with cunning fine tipped brushes
I'm talking about embossing machines
And distressing machines
And alcoholic ink
Thermal binders, hot plastic and vinyl, heat guns,
bone folders, gellyroll pens
Appliqué
Mounting adhesive and rubber stamps
Wire and lace
Guillotine cutters, wavy and saw-toothed

Liquid pearls
Tweezers transparencies, stickles hole punchers and rhinestone rub-
ons.

(*Restore light*)

I have never been able to keep a girlfriend.

This has something to do with my misanthropic tendencies and
abiding sense of discontent, but upon closer examination and to be
perfectly crass about it, it seems to have as much to do with owning
the wrong stuff. I never could find a point of entry with the other
girls- I always had the wrong Barbie, the wrong bike, the wrong
boy, the wrong bible.

Over the years I have been collected and discarded by a number of
excellent girls and women, or maybe I'm the one who did the
discarding, it's hard to tell, the ecology in this sort of relationship is
so delicate. I'm convinced there's something off about my Ph.

That's why Debbie Harold, my best friend in fourth grade
dropped me like a plutonium pet rock in fifth. It's why Susan
Butler and Laura Baldwin turned against me in sixth (just try to
keep a threesome going in middle school). It's why I contrived to
accept Jesus Christ into my heart in the seventh grade, at the behest
of my then best friend born again Nancy Dick, but Nancy moved to
Pennsylvania, leaving me with a paperback New Testament and a
relationship with the messiah that prohibited invitations to any of
the more interesting Junior High parties.

In High School all the girls were wearing Lacoste polo shirts and
soft, wide wale corduroys in colors like sea foam, vanilla cream and
blush. They looked like a delicious assortment of candied almonds
at an Italian wedding. Vickie Grischo, whom I'd known since
kindergarten, started wearing pounds of Maybelline and at a
sleepover admitted she considered wearing her make-up to bed
when there were other girls around. Her suddenly shy face shone
with acne. I told her I thought she looked much better without the
make-up. In fact, I told her, I found her bare face beautiful. (Jesus
never took, but evangelical hyperbole was and remains irresistible.)
I told her I found her bare face beautiful and she sort of stopped
talking to me after that.

I liked the stoner girls in my high school; they were kind and vague and they laughed at my jokes. Hell, they laughed at anything. They wore blue eye pencil on the inside of their eyelids which I used to think was what made their eyes so very red, and like their boyfriends they wore Metallica and Mötley Cröe t-shirts. I never sat through a Metallica song.

But I do admire Mötley Crüe for their work in pioneering the gratuitous use of the umlaut.

The shifting of loyalties, interests, status; the wooing, the gauging of silences; the careful track kept of who has had whom and what precisely is owed: I assumed all of that would even out after high school. College. Marriage. Babies.

But adulthood in the suburbs is intricate and perverse.

A scattering of olives and martini shakers, her husband wears an absurd plaid sport coat all in fun, cocktails have come back into vogue, we should have them over *they* had *us* over, our children go to soccer together to swimming together to softball together, our daughters are best friends, decorative center pieces, really expensive vodka, Hostess gifts: candles, wine, gossip, potpourri.

Coffee in the kitchen on winter afternoons we sit, you and I, like two sit-com wives and streak each other's hair with red. I will fall in love with you and I will write you a poem but the truth is this:

(*Special poetry light*)

The truth is I probably think you're prettier than me.

The truth is I probably think I'm smarter than you.

The truth is I do not wonder what your husband looks like naked.

The truth is I do wonder what you look like naked.

The truth is I don't invite you over for dinner often because you're a chef and I'm ashamed of my cooking.

The truth is the poem I write for you while standing in line at the grocery store will confuse you.

The truth is I don't like being referred to as "artsy."

The truth is you're going to have to work a lot harder to entertain me.

The truth is just because we've both had babies doesn't mean we're going to be friends.

The truth is I shouldn't have offered you a poem that was really really stupid, I should've offered you candles, wine, gossip, potpourri.

The truth is we will both try, honestly we will, but when I see the scrapbook supplies, I should know it's never going to work.

(back to general light)

I see you working on your scrapbook and I'm enchanted. Your lips are lightly glossed and you are warmly lit from the tiffany lamp. You place a cork workboard over your unmarred dining room table. While our children watch your TV you turn the heavy pages for me.

"ALL BOY!" shouts the caption beneath a photo of your youngest. He is an imp in an oversized baseball cap and look! Look how you have wound an old sneaker string around his picture to create a frame, and there is a cunning shower of gold stamped stars dribbling from one corner because his team is called the Comets! And the ribbons are blue because his eyes are blue *but mostly because he is a Winner.* And there is your daughter in toe shoes with "GIRL POWER!" emblazoned in magenta, and next to her is a ticket stubs from her time as a snow tree angel in The Joffrey Nutcracker, and the tickets are wrapped in netting with fabric rosebuds attached and there are cards from the various bouquets she received and a raveling from the Sugar Plum Fairy's Pointe shoe.

My daughter was a snow tree angel in the Joffrey Nutcracker.

I don't have a single picture. Neither of us even knows where the program is.

And suddenly it doesn't matter that my daughter is smarter than your daughter, and funnier than your daughter and in spite of her morbid tendencies or perhaps because of them, emotionally healthier than your daughter.

That doesn't matter.

What matters is I don't have a Sissex Machine.

I don't know what a Sissex Machine is.

But apparently you can't do any serious scrapbooking without one.

And if I could do this thing, make a book like this with stickers and stars, all joyous and celebratory, a chronicle of our lives so far, as slick as an advertisement from Real Simple Magazine, my sons wouldn't care less but *my daughter* would love me more and she's the one I have to woo, to win to romance, the boys are puppy brained and breastfed and they love me but lets face it anything with boobs will do, it's the girl who looks at me the way all girls have ever looked at me, with measuring tape eyes, with a shrug and a smile and,

LISTEN YOU!

Our daughters are in love with each other in that way that is only allowed when you are in the fourth grade and soon it happens that your daughter drops my daughter like a plutonium pet rock and I will spend many nights holding my daughter while she cries over this first heartbreak and reflecting that just because my daughter desperately wants to be friends with your stinking daughter doesn't mean I need to be friends with you, it's not you I desire its *that book,* that book of sunshine and accomplishment, brilliantly *illustrating* a state of neurosis that it is meant to *disguise.*

It's a funeral.

It's a chance to direct and attend your own funeral, to illustrate your own self-indulgent eulogy and wallow in it.

I could never make a book like this; none of my neurosis are sub-textual. And there are no rubber stamps with cute sayings about borderline agoraphobia and how the never-ending pursuit of self-worth sure can fuck with interpersonal relationships. There's no place in a book like this for that most generous of gestures; my husband's index finger, gently pushing his penis down so that he may direct his urine stream into the toilet.

A Cleveland Steamer is not simply the act of taking a shit on your lover's chest. One must then plop down on said partner's chest and roll back and forth using the buttocks to create a wallow for the purpose of enjoying a product of one's own making.

THE END

Girl Be Heard: Unplugged

Written and Performed by Mariaisabel Zweig, Ruby Gerber, Betsy Perez, Dinae Anderson, Melanie Thompson, Aya Abdelaziz, Shira Spiel and Sara Ravid, Breani Michele
Devised in Workshops lead by Winter Miller
Edited by Winter Miller with additional editing by Rachel Lerner-Ley and Jessica Greer Morris
Stage Managed by Lauren Arneson
Directed by Ashley Marinaccio
www.girlbeheard.org

GREETINGS by MariaIsabel Zweig
THE WAR by Sara Ravid
MIRRORS by Betsy Perez
HOPE IS NOT ENOUGH by Shira Spiel
FAMILY OWNED by Betsy Perez
GIRL BE HEARD* by Breani Michele
UNTITLED by Ruby Gerber
SELLING YOUR BODY by Melanie Thompson
BABIES IMAGINING BABIES by Betsy Perez
LOVE CAME by Ruby Gerber
I WAS UGLY AND I KNEW IT by Dinae Anderson
WHEN THE WORLD IS WEAK Aya Abdelaziz
I WRITE by Melanie Thompson
GIRL BE HEARD* (Reprise) by Breani Michele

*denotes original song

Greetings

by MariaIsabel Zweig

Come out, come out.
Where ever you are.
I came all the way to corporate Starbucks to say
Welcome to the hot pink triangle
Welcome to eyes wide open.

Greetings to the
CHUBBY CHICKS
with
HAIRY PITS
and a
PUSSY CAT
to match!
to the
CONQUERORS
CONQUISTADORS
of public space
the maps.
Me llamo
Frida Kahlo
Dorothy Parker
Sojourner Truth.
inventor of
THE BIRTH CONTROL
the vibrator, masturbation
FEMININE YOUTH!
My boots have walked through Ecuador
Mexico, the Taliban, vermouth.
And I've come all the way to corporate Starbucks
to have a talk with YOU.
Did you have the hot pink dream yet?

CAST
No.
Aya

(steps forward in secret)
Yes.
MariaIsabel
The one where you live life awake?
Where rice pudding tastes great.
Mira chica honey bun,
my moustache is mythical
if you go to the pier in the West Village,
which you will
every happy human goes eventually
with eyes wide open, eyebrows hit the roof
you'll see my face on the water fountains
where my transgender transgiveafuck
lower their plump little lips
to suck up the fluidity
of a multi-talented spectrum
mujeres with the hot wax for who?
Ladies, before you do anyone
do yourself in your room
drink your mocha hot (say it to Aya)
with the whipped cream
MORE whipped cream
burn your thinsperation,
your thinspo
and here,
take my combat boots
you're in the hot pink triangle baby
it's a war zone in here
dykes like me
don't know what they're getting into
when they fall in love
with a soft skinned someone
every date to the movies
is a revolution
every kiss on the subway
is as loud as the junction reggae
blasting in the street

floating up to the classroom
every kiss is a patti smith Gloria
dykes pay consequences
our psyches are up for evaluation
but at least the front lobby's got
rice pudding.
Come out, come out.
Where ever you are.
Welcome to the hot pink triangle
Welcome to eyes wide open.

The War

by Sara Ravid

Character: GIRLS 1, 2 and 3
1 on SR, 2 in SC, 3 on SL- stare straight into imaginary mirrors

GIRL 2: I'm doing it again. Right before I shower, I take off all my clothes, go to the bathroom mirror, and stare.

GIRL1: My ass is too flat

GIRL 3: My boobs are too big

GIRL 2: And my stomach. I'm constantly at war with my stomach.

GIRL 1: I try to fight it. I cut out everything.

GIRL 3: Meat

GIRL 2: Sugar

GIRL 1: Bread

GIRL2: Fat

ALL: Everything.

GIRL 3: But it's still winning. In the mirror, I touch and pinch it. My reflection is unforgiving.

GIRL 2: I have pretty eyes, I think.

GIRL 3: But you're fat, the mirror answers

GIRL 1: I have good cheekbones, I think. But you're horribly,

GIRL 3: Disgustingly,

ALL: FAT.

GIRL 2: My eyes fill and I step into the shower. My hot tears are swallowed by even hotter water pouring over me.

GIRL 1: I imagine the water clears away not just the germs and the dirt of the day, but the pounds on the scale that just won't disappear.

GIRL 3: I touch my stomach and my hips, feel the smooth, wet skin underneath my fingertips.

GIRL 2: I close my eyes and breathe the steam in deeply, and as I let it out, I hope tomorrow I'll have the strength to battle myself again.

GIRL 3: And maybe

GIRL 1: Just maybe

GIRL 2: Maybe

ALL: I'll win.

Mirrors

by Betsy Perez

DIANA: Wow, you're so beautiful *(in awe)* you got ma's looks

LUCY: Dee, really? We both got her looks now c'mon and do this face. I can't understand how you are such a natural at this, I can't tell the eyeshadow from the blush.

DIANA: Ha! Natural is what I wish for, practice is what I call it, faking it till they believe is even better.

Lucy: No hangups, remember?

DIANA: Can I ask you something, what makes you a woman? What does that mean?

LUCY: *(surprised/confused)* ummm,

DIANA: Well, is it your breast? Your vagina?

LUCY: Well, that fact that I could have children, ummm my curves, my long hair, my-

DIANA: *(cutting LUCY off)* Some women can't even have kids; hell some are flat chested Lucy... Your curves? What the hell does that mean, so because my silhouette lines up with a row of bricks I'm not a woman and you can always buy hair

LUCY: Jesus Diana! I feel like one, I just know that, I AM ONE.

DIANA: Exactly, Lucy. It's in how you feel, but it seems like you have to first look like one to earn such privileges. It's what you know is real inside of you, right? So, why am I selling ass to buy 'mones'

LUCY: Mones?

DIANA: Hormones girl, like estrogen? Ive been buying estrogen off dealers since I was 15. Ive been trying look like a "real woman" for almost three years now! Upper east side pumping parties getting $2 silicone shots on my hips, my cheeks, rounding my face to make my nose look smaller, i could barely breath. I'm like an art project trying to blend in. The cement in my thighs is hardening, a constant reminder of what the world excepts me not to be, that's heavier than any rock I'm literally carrying inside. I'm tired of the stares when i walk into the women's bathroom and the harassment in the male ones. I'm sick of being asked were you born a man? Well you have a dick, don't you? So why did you check female? You clearly are a man... But luz, what makes either, I've always felt like a girl, I now feel like a woman. I'm a woman, when will they see that.

Hope Is Not Enough

by Shira Spiel

I feel so uncontrollable... So irrational... From the tagged Facebook photo. The one posted yesterday. You were so adorable. Your hair was so fluffy and you haven't lost all your baby fat off your cheeks yet... I can't believe you were my age in that picture; you looked too young for only 19.

It wasn't the picture though- it was who posted it… And how it was posted. Alone- hanging in Facebook space- not even in an album with other older pictures. Why would she do that? To say, "hey we knew you back then, you can't cut us out"? Or maybe even "I miss you"?

The friendship with your exes, just the thought that there might be a particle of your emotions still tied to them makes my stomach churn… the thought that you still care about what they think or if they're happy… that you genuinely enjoy their company. How can I not think that that happiness they give you, even a plutonic coffee catch-up, is something you want and need and something that I cannot possibly give to you.

I'm just sick of crying, of judging my reflection. Of nights sitting wondering if I am as good as her- if I could possibly be better? I'm so sick of the days of being afraid that you might get sick of me or grow tired of who I am.

You give me no reason to believe this. You are so understanding- you are so good to me. You make me feel so loved and so whole and just so at ease with myself. I love you. When you are here with me these fears become immaterial.

But they always come back! I can't stop myself from spinning after I see these reminders. After she calls to check up or to get dinner with you. Why? What is the point? You obviously ended for a reason.

I tell myself to look at you and know you are mine now, and know that the past has no power over us and that you will be here for months and years to come. But, I'm sure she felt the same. I'm sure you both did. So how can I be sure it's true if it was believed so strongly before? How can I be sure I'm good enough to keep?

How can I completely trust in something that nobody can ever really know?

Incest 101
Family Owned and Operated

by Betsy Perez

At age nine, I was too much body for my age. I don't know if it was the platanos or the quest frito, but this girl was busting out of everything when I got my period.
"Maaaami, toy sangrado de mi cosa,"

All I heard back was "Que?! Mira muchacha no relaje."
I swear I thought my mother was going to rush me to the emergency room but all she said was, "Ya eres señorita, a young women."
Keep in mind, I'm nine and here is this part of me that I kind of, sort of knew existed only cause I peed through it, is now bleeding.
My mother and I hadn't had "the talk." The one about becoming a woman. About how to safeguard "it." Not let anyone touch "it." It was so confusing. Especially since everyone was touching "it" but me.

At five, I opened up shop without even realizing. It was a family owned business, I guess. Cousins and a very involved Uncle Freddy, took pride in my shop. Polished me up, every week... Being sexually abused so young for so long became normal. I thought that's how you relate, how you show love. So I started very young, like 1st grade young, sucking Lina Santos' tits in the bathroom. I was taught that everyone's first sexual experiences are supposed to be with your cousins. Los primos se priman is what we call it in Latino culture. It's a saying we have for incest. I don't know how true that is for you, but it was for me.

Every weekend, my family would get together for dominoes, bingo and cards. I conveniently found myself scheming situations that involved touching one of my cousins, Lorena or Cynthia. Or my neighbor_____ (name) (who was only _____ years old), the neighbors pride and joy. I always was the initiator; it felt great.

Uncle Freddy taught me everything I knew. He asked my mother every weekend to let me come over to play...allegedly with cousin Lucy but she was never there. Uncle Freddy would ever so subtly trace the straps of my tank top. Then he'd ask me to come see something in his bedroom. Then touch me, have sex with me. He would catch me in the cuts. Rub me down quickly, our "quickies" he called it. He was my mentor. I learned the art of luring and manipulation. I learned to say"It's ok, no one is looking." To reassure Lorena and Cynthia -- " I won't tell. I promise." I hated it but loved the control, the only one I had. The control over someone else's body. Uncle Freddy taught me well. It's Incest 101.

Girl Be Heard*

by Breani Michele

Verse one
I feel you girl I can feel your pain
You ain't the only one with issues don't be ashamed
A different girl is getting raped every day
There is a lot of men with daughters they don't claim
Listen I'm a girl just like you
Have a moment that I think I won't get through
Sometimes I'm insecure I don't know what to do
I fight the devil so **the** negative won't get
I talk for a reason
I want to make a change speaking for what I believe **in**
Empower the girl that's getting bullied
Confront the ones doing the teasing

What about the girl that cried **her**self to sleep
Single mom no food to eat
What about the girl **that** joined the **gang** to survive
She finally felt safe and could sleep at night
What about the lonely **rich** girl
Material girl
No genuine family of friends
Everyone around her acts pretend
So she takes a couple pills so her life could end
Is this how they want our youth
Society **blind** eyes they don't see the true
They say they're helping these girls
But they show no proof

GBH girls that's my crew
We might teach you a lesson or 2
Cause every girl goes through their obstacles
Every girl is a strong soldier
So stand up and salute

Chorus
Don't let nobody tell you that you can't do that
Don't let nobody tell you that you can't do this
You want to make a change then take the risk
Speak out loud
Girl be heard
Hey hey hey
Girl be heard
Hey hey Hey
Girl Be heard

Verse two
15 and Pregnant feeling like an outcast
Carrying for a child is not an easy task
Mom kicked her out said she's fast
Friends judge her she don't go to class
She stays out in the street
Because she think it's going to care
Prostituting Just so she can buy her baby food clothes and footwear
Girl I come commend you
I'm here to wipe your tears
I speak loud and proud
So all my females could hear
I'm ready to go to war
I'm in on all My gear
This world is very Blurry
I'm here to make it clear
Call me a contact

Does am the one they contact
To liberate the generation and make an impact
Impact their soul

I tell them To just be you
Beauty varies depending on Who be holds
Whoa yo there I go
Preaching facts with my feminist flow
Shout to Rosie O'Donnell
Speaking for gay pride
She's a role model
She would be proud of me
Cause I'm giving these girl a chance to see
They don't have to follow the women in the magazines
They can be individuals spread their wings and be free

Chorus
Don't let nobody tell you that you can't do that
Don't let nobody tell you that you can't do this
You want to make a change then take the risk
Speak out loud
Girl be heard
Hey hey hey
Girl be heard
Hey hey Hey
Girl Be heard

I'm Not OK

by Ruby Gerber

(NOTE: What happened to santa? To the word anorexia?)

At times I tell myself I'm not okay.
I'm lost.
Misplace in an uncaring, impatient world
Hidden by expectations and the hysteria of life.
My voice has been stolen, and I can't find it.
My once rooted strong feet seem to have been uprooted, chopped
And boiled in a **savory** stew
The arms with which I had once extended upward are short and no
longer able to reach the sky.
Shouting creates more silence, than being quiet.
I have learned this from experience.

Sadly.
Though the waves of fear and discouragement wash over my body
everyday.
I stand strong.
Words sometimes twist and sting me,
Yet I found their beauty.
The world might seem like a dark place,
But it's not.
The world is just as lost as me.
It is spinning,
Seeming to stay in place,
But never still
I don't mind being lost or uprooted,
Because I know I am not alone.
Though my voice has been hidden by my own insecurity
A new voice emerges
An unchanging and powerful voice that can't be taken

Selling Your Body

by Melanie Thompson

<u>**I was trafficked at age 9. Forced to sell my**</u> body.

Where do I begin? It's a live or die situation. Having a man that u r
not physically attracted to touching on u and licking and kissing on
u to THIER point of satisfaction yet u lay there in agony thinking
silently "it's only temporary, you can do this." A random man
whispering all the things that the person that should b having a lock
on ur heart should b whispering. You have the Indian with his
scratchy wannabe fresh cut beard and that makes every one of his
"dates" his temporary "wife." The Mexican who can't speak a lick of
anything but spanish yet knows how to French kiss and stroke
faster than a black man. The spanish boy who is younger and
decent looking yet gets no female attention and is desperate for a
moment in his life where he can truthfully brag to his friends that
he finally "got some." And last but not least the old white man who
uses viagra and whose age restricts him from having the ability to
even think about sex, yet is filthy stankin' rich and irresistible. Its
not a life that most of us choose. I for one was put into it forcefully,

but once in it u realize the reality of the perception of womanhood to men that the media fails to make known. U are a piece of meat. The way that men can devour a steak is the way that men want to devour u. Eat up all the meat and then discard the bone. The worthless bone that no one no longer wants. The valueless item that just lingers around until the trash is taken out. If us women never had pussies there would be no value to us. Ain't nothing to chase after or attempt to impress. Useless. In this life, that's how u r viewed. It's like u allow someone to take control of u in exchange for u trying to b in control of urself.

It's consensual rape. Laying on your back or kneeling on your knees just so that you can survive. You give yourself to support yourself and your family however internally do not permit abuse and scars and pain that are not self inflicted. You are not necessarily seeking the emotional stability from this party from an encounter but more like financial stability. Yet while most are blinded by the monetary gain almost always guaranteed at the end they forget to include the emotional downfall and mental abuse they will suffer into their thoughts. The confusion ur soul will suffer due to the contemplation between ur mind and ur body. One saying this is gross and wrong and I cant take this and the other erect and continuously lubricating at the sense of ur slightest touch. You ask urself do I like this? Is this actually right? No it can't be right but wait I am still wet. I am disgusted and I feel dirty. I feel like I have rolled in dirt until it was so embedded into my skin that u would think it was a part of my complexion. But at the same time my pussy is enjoying it? My exterior is contradicting my inner self. God only knows how I should react. But now ur left with this body on top of u sweating an panting and making noises towards u and u on the bottom with no type of mutual attraction and scared to death. I said no once. He wanted it raw. He told me to calm down as he pushed and held my body down against the bed by my neck and whispered u are my girlfriend. And when my screams got louder he shouted back and said stop acting. I cried. How dare you accuse me of acting when u see that ur physically hurting me. I guess that's what u men do. You don't give a **fuck**. They want one thing and one thing only. I keep thinking ur a stupid girl; a stupid stupid

stupid girl. U shouldn't have went over to his house. U shouldn't have trusted his facade as being naive as a foreigner and taken ur clothes off. That's where this all started. Maybe if u kept ur head on the right track u wouldn't have got urself into this mess. U wouldn't even think about boys at the age u were. But unfortunately I was subjected to growing up faster. So now Im left with the question. Now what? What am I gonna do? Who have I become? What is left of me? I understand that these rapes and this life wasn't my fault but how bad of a contribution has it made to my current personality? Who am I really?

Babies Imagining Babies

by Betsy Perez

Mark twain said," the difference between a lie and a cat , is that a cat has nine lives." I wish I was the cat cause that would mean I'd stop at nine. That my life would be one big lie instead of **countless** ones Dispersed among friends from **various** stages of my life. **See in my high school, pregnancy is a fashion statement, so I got tangled in a big lie.**

GIRL 1: So how's your son?

LISA: Oh, ummm he's good. Big. Gotta go

(*pause*)

See, to you I am

GIRL 1: Lisa

GIRL 2: 22, from the south Bronx

GIRL 3: But now living in manhattan

GIRL 1: Lesbian

GIRL 2: Not bisexual

GIRL 3: This is the year I have been the most honest**...well that is Until someone caught me the BIG LIE and** asked about my son.

GIRL 2: Son?

GIRL 1: I thought you were gay?

GIRL 3: You have a kid?

When I was in the 6th grade. **I** was dying to be got pregnant.

GIRL 1: 16 in the 6th grade, long black hair

GIRL 2: A body only 16 year olds who are having sex have

GIRL 1: Most of us girls

GIRL 2: 10 and 11 year old girls

GIRL 1: had just started bra training, our bras snapped in the front

GIRL 3: Hers on her back.

GIRLS: uh humm!
    And for whatever reason, i got pregnant too. It was genius! I
    researched pregnancies, bordeline obsessed

GIRL 1: womenshealth.com

GIRL 2: webmd.com

GIRL 3: babycenter.com

GIRL 2: Wikipedia

I made up a boyfriend, victor, he was deadbeat and uninvolved,
believable for this day and age. All of this at ten years old, can you
believe it?

GIRLS: I know!

Then whala! I started to little by little let my belly stick out, I
virtually had no concept on the growth of a pregnant woman's belly
but I figured something was something. I still had baby fat so ill had
to do was practice making my stomach as stiff as possible, harder
then it looks. And the third trimester was just a bitch to pull off! My
friends eventually bought it and teachers ignored it. The girls would
touch my belly and either I was really good or they were very
oblivious but I would pop my belly out so they can feel the baby
move.

GIRLS: It was genius!

Thank god my god mother was pregnant just in time for me to claim her baby. We are also first cousins so, Alicia looked just like me. Everyone really believed me then. I paraded her, I was in labor for 37 hours over the winter brake and was back in school on the January 2.
What I didn't know was that babies get older and so do lies. I thought people would forget and I'd be able to reinvent myself

GIRLS: forget the past

GIRL 1: but the lie grew, beyond me.

GIRL 3: people who knew people

GIRL 2: who knew me, knew about Alicia

The lie was the truth for many. I kept it up and continues to lie. I had a second pregnancy in high school. This one, no one ignored and my counselor was extremely concerned with the kind of life I would be able to provide to my "son" if I was unable to graduate. My mother caught up with my truancy and my lie one inevitable morning.

COUNSELOR: how is your grandson?

MOTHER: grandson? I'm sorry I don't think I understand.

COUNSELOR: Jeremiah, he must be about two months. Lisa just told us she had him in August.

MOTHER: I'm sorry to tell you but that isn't true and she has spread this lie to several people and I don't understand why.

GIRL 3: It was the attention that made me do it!

Home wasn't panning out, suicide attempts, molestation, hyper-sexuality my reality was crashing down on me. Every now i then I run into people who ask about my child or my children. All i wanted was to be loved, even if the person that I assigned the job to love me was, imaginary.

Love Came

by Ruby Gerber

Love came into my life, unexpectedly, almost unwilling

He (or she?) it crept **his** way through the crevices, all sticky and slimy from past injuries. **Johnny Sarnow** pierced his way into my skull, leaving a gap for other emotions to flood their way in, on the long journey down my veins and around my brain deep into the nadir of my heart.

Love brought with it a cascade of feelings, like envy, and longing,

And the sneaky essence of happiness.

For the first time love allowed me,

To take a deep breathe on a fall day and not look at all the death brought on by the coming frost,

No it allowed me to look at fall as a beautiful parting of the warmer months,

And a majestic welcoming of the cold

Love managed to kill something in me,

That dark longing place that some call depression

Love drained all thoughts of death and sadness away with its florescent lights, beaming artificial illumination into the corners that usually don't see day

Love reels you in like a giant fish,

Flopping about,

Helpless to the sharpen hook

And if it is neglected it rots and shrivels away

It leaves you broken,

With pieces that you knew once fit together,

But now seem ill placed

Love came into my life out of nowhere,

It hit me with a gust of its perfume as it was leaving,

Crippling something inside me, which it had initially sparked.

But I must say thank god for love,

Because without it what would I be hunting for?

What would I listen to on the radio?

So love entered my body, filling each inch with its bittersweet melodic tales

And once it left I sat and waited for it to come back.

I Was Ugly and I Knew It

by Dinae Anderson

When I was six, I thought I could swim instead of just dropping to the bottom of the pool. I was one of those poor kids from Harlem who got shipped to the some white family's home in Pennsylvania with the "Fresh Air Fund." They were perfectly nice but had no idea I didn't know how to swim. I remember holding a big pink noodle in their backyard pool and next thing you know, I was drowning and had to be saved.

A few years later, I turned into a nerd. Picture me at 9. This little girl who studied Bill Clinton's autobiography and encyclopedias as if they were as simple to understand as multiplication problems. So small and frail with big buck teeth... you'd think it was cute.

And you'd never know I was drowning. Depression was the biggest secret I ever kept. You'd see the happiest 4th grader in the world. Ready to conquer the world. Ready to learn with glee. See, it's funny...because no one back then would have known. Guessed my secret.

Nine years old, and I'm banging my head on the white walls of my bedroom for hours on end. With each thud I could temporarily dull the pain. My head ached, but no major damage, and it did job.

Constant teasing and bullying at school made it all worse. They beat me up cause I was a nerd. And different. And little. And most importantly, because I was ugly. I was ugly and I knew it. Mother's words of encouragement that I was beautiful and those kids were jealous were no watch for their chants of "Beaver" or "You're mad ugly!" I was never enough.

And because I wasn't enough, I had to escape. Every year, something new to help me get through school.

At age 10, the kids at school said my hair was ugly so I cut it. It looked horrendous but they left me alone. Began overeating at 11 after being asked if I was pregnant in front of the whole lunchroom.

Had a classic emo stage at 13 which I thought would save me. Painted my nails black and listened to rock. This only only brought on more humiliation when a boy in my homeroom, yelled "Hey Beaver, you're afucking nerd!" in my face. "Bitch, you're fucking ugly, you hear me?" And the punishment he got for that? Was having to write a meaningless letter of apology to me that I ripped to shreds. And when his friend threw a history textbook at my head, I decided take matters into my own hands. I swallowed a handful of Motrin. It turned out it wasn't enough to take me down but ended me in the hospital. What a poor excuse of a first suicide attempt before eighth grade graduation. Mom thought it was a stunt for attention. So once again, my secret was safe.

Finally to my relief, high school arrived. I thought people would change. That I would finally be pretty to someone. Wrong. Instead, "Beaver" became "Buck Tooth Betty" after it was decided by some popular, Bronx bred girls I was a whore for wearing fishnets to school. And of course, I was ugly. And now, fat. So I dealt with my depression once more, this time with an eating disorder that left me at 98 pounds by the time I was 15. Mom tried to force feed me nasty ass Spam so I stopped that.

A purge did not end the ugliness. Did not end the name-calling. Did not end the bullying. So I started a dance with a friend called a blade. I did the tango all over my arms, did pirouettes on my breasts, and fox-trotted up and down my thighs. The sight of blood was the greatest feeling. My most beautiful of coping mechanisms. And by the summer, there was no stopping me. I was drinking anything I could get my hands on and smoking weed but mostly cutting. Cutting during work. Cutting after work. Cutting during dinner. Cutting was my best friend. It emphasized my ugliness and I embraced it with open arms.

By the time I started junior year, I was a bloody mess. Mother finally paid attention and took all of my friends, my precious blades, from me.

So I just got another from the toolbox in the kitchen and dug into my face this time, in addition to my body. When mom broke into the bathroom, I was bleeding everywhere. Mother took the blade from my hand. *(pause)*

My will to live was somewhere on the floor. Ready to be mopped away. On the mirror, to be windexed out of existence. On my journal too. My life line. My little book of secrets… no more. Two days later, I had an awakening. That although it was going to be hell to swim from the bottom, I didn't want to keep drowning myself in this misery. I still felt ugly but there was that little six year old girl inside of me who wanted to be saved. This time however, I had to be the one to save me from myself.

When the World is Weak

by Aya Abdelaziz

I'd like to make the steps to my own tango
Dance in the divide between Busta Rhyme and Ani Difranco
I know that I can write my own
A seed in the soot of this barren limbo
At least I have a life

Though
I was shot by a lie my own president dealt
As I bled my own mind didn't know it fell
Rotting like a fruit dying like leaves
Plucked
From the Sycamore tree of my soul
Sucked
Changing color to the rhythm of it all
Art?
Well that's what I thought
And I'm told not to speak
But I can't shut up

Because

This is the fury of the West dropped

To the beat of the Middle East
Drawled where the cold and hot meet
Cooked in the womb of a lover's mystery

This is a refusal to repeat
An oppression of two centuries
When they kill the drone kills me
And all I use to keep me free

VERSE 2

I like to paint my fears a dollar-bill green
Remind me what the real nightmares are made of
I cover my eyes in my undercover sleep
Console me away from the war I was born

Into the ocean I dive
Followed by the nation of an overgrown lie
Dip your toes into where I've cried
Melted to maximize another piece of capital

This is the fury of a woman (produced)
This is a girl misused
This is the clash of cultures bruised
This is a love consumed *(swallow)*

This is a body marred
This is the sister of another girl scarred
This is a longing breaking through
This is me
Who are you

I Write

by Melanie Thompson

I write
Because I know that someone is going to read it. Because I know
that they will listen to what my thoughts are trying to say. All the
things I feel but don't have the courage to articulate.
I sing

Because I know that my voice can tell a story. Grab someone's attention then demand their comprehension. Because the only way that I can speak my thoughts is through a melody. Where a high pitch and a low pitch represent silent emotions and a crack in my voice represents silent defeat.

I dance

Because I know my body can send a message, and it displays to people when my heart here skips a beat. Left kick or a right kick to a Left turn to a pivot means that my conscious is going wild and I am drifting off my feet.

I act

Cuz I am kind and can feel others emotions. I put myself in their shoes and can feel what they're going through. Suffering, happiness, anger or distress, I act out their problems to make a change before they rest.

I eat

To fill my body up with lots of energy, to keep my mind pumping and to give the world what's left of me.

I cry

To give the air the worst parts of my pain and release all of the hurt that was captured inside my veins and

I sex

Because I need a persons consolation; need the validation from a woman or a man, from one person to a band, and they accept who I am, and then they call me beautiful while walking hand in hand With me...

Because I know that I am real unique, a special treat for everyone that anyone can see. From my curvaceous hips to my nose to my lips. My beauty is skin deep and by a rose its been kissed. Just some of my characteristics to show my inner skin and make you wanna get to know the me that's deep within.

Girl Be Heard (Reprise)

CHORUS] X 2
When the world is weak
I sit down and pray
Sip at frustration till it fades away

If it's a lie I'll still believe
And I dare you to try to break through my faith

I know the going gets hard
But it also gets gone
Grab at the clock till I hear the alarm
And though I'm dying from the wait
I dare you to try to break through my patience

I dare you to try to break my patience

The End

ROSANNA UAMAGIWA ALFARO, *Sailing Down the Amazon.* Her play *Before I Leave You* was produced by the Huntington Theater in 2011. Her other full-length plays were produced by Pan Asian Repertory, East West Players, the Magic Theater and New Theatre. Many of her short plays are anthologized; they appeared in venues such as La MaMa , the Edinburgh Fringe Festival, and the Boston Theater Marathon. She wrote and narrated the documentary, *Japanese American Women: A Sense of Place* (Leita Hagemann, dir.). She was a 2011 Massachusetts Cultural Council Artist Fellow.

LISA BRUNA, *Redemption,* lives, in South Florida, where she's written and directed plays for numerous theatres throughout Palm Beach County. She is Co-Founder/Producing Partner of an independent theatre collaborative, Palm Beach PlayMakers, which produces a semi-annual short-play showcase called BOXer SHORTS, in which five of Lisa's plays have been featured: *Chillers, Cuts, Upshot, Redemption* and *Yellow.* Three of her newest plays, *Terrance, Heavy Lifting* and *Invasion,* will be produced in the next line-up. Lisa is thrilled, honored and forever grateful that her play, *Redemption,* was included ⁊ and even won an Audience Favorite designation! ⁊ in the 13th Annual Estrogenius Festival. Lisa's book, theatre and film credits, can be found online at www.lisabruna.com.

TRISH COLE, *Life on Mars,* is a tomboy poet and playwright whose work often explores the intersection of social construct, gender, and identity. Her stage plays have been produced in New York, Chicago, Seattle, San Francisco, and regionally in Maryland. Trish is the recipient of the 2010 MCTF Excellence in Original Script Award, the author of the 2011 Maryland Community Theater Festival winner, a 2011 Bakeless Literary Prize Finalist, and the recipient of the 2013 MCTF Outstanding Original Play Award. Her website is www.trishcole.net.

ALESSANDRA DRAPOS, *Tea With Vivien Leigh,* is an actor, comedian, and playwright. Graduate of Adelphi University and the London Dramatic Academy, she wrote/performed *Tea with Vivien Leigh* in England beside acclaimed artistic director of Theatre Royal Stratford East's, Philip Hedley. Her drama was performed again in NYC, under the direction of Marlee Koenigsberg; courtesy of Estrogenius. Alessandra also collaborated with award winning director Andrew Block, as well as True False Theatre; receiving the 2013 Planet Connections nomination for outstanding supporting actress. She immersed herself in improv at New York's Upright Citizens Brigade and Chicago's Second City. She currently resides in New York.

GINA FEMIA, *Happily Never Ever.* Her work has been presented as a part of The New Ideas Festival in Toronto, Dixon Place's HOT! Festival, The Women Center Stage Festival (New Georges, *Just Do It!*), HERE Arts Center (New York Madness, *Occupy Sandy*), The United Solo Festival, The Short Play By Women's Festival in Columbia, MO (featured playwright), The Horse & Cart Play Offs in Denver, and the Estrogenius Festival (Sola Voce). She is an affiliated artist of New Georges. Semi-Finalist: The Inkwell 2013, Princess Grace Award 2012, Spotlight On: Solo Writing 2012. MFA, Sarah Lawrence College, Lipkin Award in playwriting.

SETH FREEMAN, *Jumping In.* His plays have been presented around the world. He has worked in print (*New York Times, Wall Street Journal, Los Angeles Times, Huffington Post*), screen and television, creating, most recently, the series *Lincoln Heights.* His journalism, screen and television writing has won numerous awards. He serves on boards of the Rape Foundation, UCLA Health System, and traveled recently to Guatemala with the Pacific Council on International Policy investigating violence against women in that country.

MARIA GABRIELE, *Cheap Chicken,* is a writer of drama and fiction, a performer, and a translator (of all things German) based in Brooklyn. Her plays and monologues have been produced in numerous NYC venues and festivals, as well as across the ocean, in Austria. She is a founding member of The Verbal Supply Company, which is dedicated to spreading the literary word audibly and in all its variety.

SHARON GOLDNER, *Bazookas.* Her award-winning plays have been produced at: Hand-to-Mouth Players (NY); Rochester Repertory Theatre (MN); Future Tenant (PA); Manhattan Repertory Theatre; twice at Run of the Mill Theater (MD); twice at North Avenue Play Series (MD); twice at Fells Point Corner Theater (MD); twice at The Women's Theatre Project (FL); Longwood University (VA); Love Creek Productions (NYC); Stage Q (WI); Modern-Day Griot Theatre Company (NY); and NYC Short Play Lab. Several monologues are in Smith & Kraus' *Best Female Monologues 2013.* Sharon is a member of Dramatists Guild.

LYNDA GREENE, *Sol,* is a NYC-based playwright and actor. Most recently, Lynda's one-act play "Clementine" was featured in Wide Eyed Theater's 2011 Festival of Women Playwrights in NYC and was a finalist the 2011 Tennessee Williams One-Act Playwriting Contest in New Orleans. Her play "Unthymely" was produced by Verses Theater Lab and Manhattan Repertory Theatre. As an actor, Lynda has worked with NJ Repertory Company, NJ Shakespeare, and NYC's Ensemble Studio Theater. Lynda studied acting at NYC's Maggie Flanigan Studio and is a graduate of Rutgers University, with degrees in Theater Arts and English. Lynda has also studied Sketch Writing at the People's Improv Theater in NYC.

LISA KENNER GRISSOM, *Orangutan and Lulu. Her play, Tattoo You* (National 10-Minute Play Award winner, The Kennedy Center American College Theater Festival), has been seen by audiences in Washington D.C., Boston, New York and Los Angeles. *Tattoo You* was also produced by The Samuel French Off Off Broadway Festival and has been selected for publication in an upcoming anthology. *the girls* (Boston Theatre Marathon), *Orangutan & Lulu* (Estrogenius Festival), MOTHERLAND (semi-finalist: Jewish Plays Project),*Chambers* (finalist: O'Neill National Playwrights Conference, The Lark, WordBRIDGE; semi-finalist: Ashland New Play Festival, PlayPenn). Her work has been presented and/or developed at The Clurman Theater, Manhattan Theatre Source, SWAN Day Boston, Blank Theatre, Road Theatre Company, Theatre of NOTE, Theatricum Botanicum. B.A. Wesleyan University; MFA Lesley University. Member: Dramatist Guild, Fell Swoop Playwrights, The Playwrights Union.

PATRICIA HENRITZE, *Destiny*, is a writer, director, and teacher focused on new works and collaborations. She is currently the Creative Director for LIFE SENTENCE, a music project inspired by Clarence Harrison, the first man exonerated by the GA Innocence Project. Favorite past collaborations include: *PROXIMITY*, with Nicole Livieratos; *Antony+Cleopatra UNDONE*, an extreme Shakespeare adaptation; *Who's There?*, performed at the Budapest Fringe Festival. Grants include: TCG Travel Grant, Poets&Writers, Inc., Idea Capital. Patricia is a lifetime member of working Title Playwrights in Atlanta GA.

HILARY KING, *The Jennifer Bourne Identity*,lives in Atlanta, Georgia. Her plays have been produced in Atlanta, New York, Pittsburgh, Colorado, Houston, Nashville and elsewhere. She is a recipient of the 2013 Ethel Woolson Lab award. Also a poet, her poems have appeared in *The Southern Poetry Anthology V: Georgia, The Cortland Review, Blue Fifth Review, Stone Highway Review, Gertrude,* and other publications. She is a member of the Dramatist Guild and Working Title Playwrights."

CELESTE KOEHLER, *A Recipe to Remember.* In 2009, Celeste responded to the call of the NWTC to write a Ten Minute play for their upcoming festival, which resulted in the production of her first three plays, *Goodbye Avis, Chelsea's Closet* and *Collateral Damage. Goodbye Avis* was later produced by The Manhattan Theatre Source, in New York City, as part of the 2011 Estrogenius Festival. *Class Act,* a play in one act, was performed by the Berliner Grund Theatre in February, 2012. *Recipe to Remember* was inspired by those women, well known to the author, who only remember the distant past.

KIRA LAUREN, *Books Not Now,* is thrilled to be a part of the EstroGenius Festival. A graduate of NYU's Tisch, she has worked professionally as an actress in Seattle, New York, and London, where she lived for seven years. Recently, Kira began work on her greatest creation – twins Rhys and Rhiannon born in August of last year. "Dedicated to R & R – who napped long enough for me to write this play." www.kiralauren.net

CATYA MCMULLEN, *When Predator Dies,* is a Brooklyn-based playwright. Her short play, MISSED CONNECTION, recently won the 2012 Samuel French OOB Short Play Festival and was directed by Leslye Headland. She is the author of four full length plays (THE COLLECTIVE, RUBBER DUCKS AND SUNSETS, EVERYTHING IS PROBABLY GOING TO BE OKAY and ROCK ME LIKE A HURRICANE) along with numerous shorts. She is a company member of The Middle Voice Theater Company (Rattlestick Playwright's Theater) and the Educational Director for Ground UP Productions. Additionally, Catya founded the "September Challenge Brunch Series." She was a finalist for the 2013 City Theater National Award for Short Playwriting, and has been produced or developed work with The Middle Voice Theater Company (Rattlestick Playwrights Theater), Naked Angels, the Estrogenius Festival, Manhattan Repertory Theater, the TRUF, The Shelter, Ground UP Productions, Ugly Rhino, ESPA at Primary Stages and UNC Chapel Hill's Department of Dramatic Art. BA UNC Chapel Hill Dramatic Art, Creative Writing.

VIVIAN NEUWIRTH, *The Key*, *The Key* won audience favorite, Program A, receiving an encore performance. Most recent work: *NOLA, Three Plays About Home* (EstroGenius 2013). NOLA includes *Fun on the Bayou* (Studio Dante, Greenwich Street Theatre, and SOAF); published: *Best Plays of the Strawberry Festival, Best Actress Award*), *Lifeline* (Samuel French Festival), *Destination* (InGenius Festival) and *Epilogue*. *NOLA* was developed as a trilogy at The Playwrights Lab at the Neighborhood Playhouse (staged reading) and the WritersForum at MTS. Other work includes *Mardi Gras Child, Do You Know What It Means* and *The Towering Dead*. Acting credits include appearances at The Kennedy Center, Goodman, Minetta Lane, Barter, The York, EST, Metropolitan Playhouse, Alonquin, ArcLight and Abingdon. Native of New Orleans. Graduate of Juilliard. Member of The Dramatists Guild. Many thanks to MTS, Jen, Anne, Vinnie and Mary.

LAUREN PRUDEN, *Out of My Mind*, lives in NYC, where she regularly performs original monologues, and opened *Listen To Your Mother* 2013 at Symphony Space. Laura's acting work includes stage (notably opposite Ann Magnuson in Amy and David Sedaris' hit *The Book of Liz*) and screen (Law & Order: SVU, The Daily Show). She studied acting at Northwestern (BA) and CalArts (MFA), taught at Second City, and received scholarships for her writing from the New York Foundation for the Arts (2011) and Adirondack Writers Retreat (2013).

LEZLIE REVELLE, *Buying the Farm.* Her myriad creative endeavors began at a young age. She has performed in choirs, variety shows, theatre productions, coffee houses, fairs and festivals. Her plays have been successfully produced in the Midwest and on both coasts. As a singer, songwriter, playwright and poet, Lezlie comments on the human experience and the divinity found within us all. Find out more at www.lezlierevelle.com.

CYNTHIA ROBINSON, *Gold Star Mother*. Awards: State University of New York Chancellor's Award for Excellence in Scholarship and Creative Activities; 2012 Calvin B. Grimes Scholar-in-Residence (NYU). Other honors: Tribeca All-Access Open Stage (2004), Best New Play IRNE nomination (*Ascension, 2006*), Thomas Barbour Memorial Playwright's Award finalist (*The Panacea*, 2008). Plays include *Nightfall* (The Fire This Time Festival); *Peola's Passing* (Samuel French OOB Theatre Festival); *Ascension* (National Black Theatre Festival; FringeNYC), *Thunder: A Musical Memoir* (FringeNYC). Cynthia is a member of The Dramatists Guild of America, Inc., writer-in-residence in the Women's Work Lab at New Perspectives Theatre Co., and Co-founder of Robinson Williams Productions.

STEPHANIE SHAW, *Octopus & If You're Feeling Blue, Paint Yourself a Different Color!*, has performed her own original solo work in theatres across Chicago and the Midwest, as well as The New York Fringe Festival and The Estrogenuis Festival. An alumni member of the Neo-Futurists, she wrote and performed regularly for *Too Much Light Makes The Baby Go Blind* and was also a theatre critic for The Chicago Reader. She is a Senior Lecturer at Columbia College Chicago, where she teaches Solo Performance among other things.